MIX
Papier aus verantwortungsvollen Quellen
Paper from responsible sources
FSC® C105338

Meenu Saihjpal

Measuring the Efficiency of Resource Use in Indian Manufacturing Industries in Pre- and Post-Reform Periods

Anchor Academic
Publishing

Saihjpal, Meenu: Measuring the Efficiency of Resource Use in Indian Manufacturing Industries in Pre- and Post-Reform Periods, Hamburg, Anchor Academic Publishing 2016

Buch-ISBN: 978-3-96067-017-9
PDF-eBook-ISBN: 978-3-96067-517-4
Druck/Herstellung: Anchor Academic Publishing, Hamburg, 2016

Bibliografische Information der Deutschen Nationalbibliothek:
Die Deutsche Nationalbibliothek verzeichnet diese Publikation in der Deutschen Nationalbibliografie; detaillierte bibliografische Daten sind im Internet über http://dnb.d-nb.de abrufbar.

Bibliographical Information of the German National Library:
The German National Library lists this publication in the German National Bibliography. Detailed bibliographic data can be found at: http://dnb.d-nb.de

Hermannstal 119k, 22119 Hamburg
http://www.diplomica-verlag.de, Hamburg 2016
Printed in Germany

FOR YOU PAPA

ABOUT THE BOOK

Looking at the development process of the economies over time, one may ask- 'Why is it that people living in some economies experience high incomes, have access to more and better quality goods and on the other hand there are economies in which people do not have access to as many goods as in other economies and even the quality of goods that they enjoy is far behind their counterparts?' 'Why is it that people living in one part of the world experience high growth rates while those living in the other parts experience low growth rates?' Although undeniably there is more than one reason for this, the one argument that has attracted the collective attention of all the scholars is the efficient use of resources. Scholars have come to believe that in the context of the rising number of the people on earth and their equally rising aspirations coupled with the scarcity of the resources used in the process of production, it becomes imperative to use the resources at hand more efficiently. Thus, the present book makes an attempt to study whether the selected Indian manufacturing industries have used resources efficiently in the pre and post-reform periods. 41 industries have been selected. The book reveals interesting insights about the problem.

ABOUT THE AUTHOR

Meenu Saihjpal is an Assistant Professor in Economics in University Institute of Legal Studies, Panjab University, Chandigarh, India. She completed her Ph.D., M.Phil and Masters in Economics from Department of Economics, Panjab University, Chandigarh, India. She has written many papers in reputed journals.

ACKNOWLEDGEMENT

This book has become possible because of the support of many people for which words are not enough. Still, I gather words to show my respect and thanks for them. First and foremost I am indebted to Dr. (Retd.). S.L.Kansra, Professor, Department of Economics, Panjab University, Chandigarh for his constant encouragement. Further, I am thankful to all my family members, friends and colleagues. Lastly, special thanks to my son, Aditya for his endurance.

CONTENTS

LIST OF TABLES

LIST OF FIGURES

ABBREVIATIONS

AU	Actual user
BIFR	Board for Industrial and Financial Reconstruction
CG	Capital Goods
CMIE	Center for Monitoring Indian Economy
CPSUs	Central Public Sector Undertakings
DRC	Domestic Resource Cost
ERP	Effective Rate of Protection
FEMA	Foreign Exchange Management Act
FERA	Foreign Exchange Regulation Act
GDP	Gross Domestic Product
IMF	International Monetary Fund
LAC	Long Run Average Cost
MNCs	Multinational Companies
MRTP	Monopolies Restrictive and Unfair Trade Practices
NAS	National Accounts Statistics
NPCs	Nominal Protection Coefficient
NSS	National Sample Survey
CSO	Central Statistics Office
PLAM	Perpetual Inventory Accumulation Method
RBI	Reserve Bank of India
TFP	Total Factor Productivity

Chapter I

INTRODUCTION

Section I Introduction

Economists have come to believe that using the resources efficiently can lead to differences in the growth rates of the economies. Efficient use of the resources is known to improve the standard of living of the people thereby increasing their welfare. However, initially 'capital' and later on 'labour' attracted the attention of the economists. The need for the efficient use of the resources was recognized as an important determinant in the growth of the economies only in the fifties. Economists believe that the developing countries, in particular, need to concentrate on improving the efficiency of the resources used as these economies have increasing number of people to feed and have relatively lesser resources at their disposal. Whenever there is a talk of efficiency of the use of the resources it means that all the resources that are used in the process of production should be used efficiently. The resources that are used in the process of production are: capital, labour, raw materials and power and fuel and the skills of the entrepreneur. Efficiency is reflected in the unit or average cost of production and in the quality of goods. The Indian industrial sector before the introduction of the reforms was characterized by the existence of numerous controls that restricted internal as well as external competition. Such controls were in the form of Industries (Development and the Regulation) Act of 1951, The Monopolies and Restrictive Trade Practices Act (1970), Foreign Exchange Regulation Act (1973), Essential Commodities Act (1955), Import Control Act, etc. In addition to these there were restrictions on the exit of the firms. As a result there were wide scale oligopolies in the Indian industrial sector, sub optimal capacities, non- availability of the better quality or cheap raw material, high power and fuel costs, lower capacity utilisation etc. Such a policy was bound to result in low efficiency of the firms in comparison to the other firms in the industry and in comparison to the firms in the foreign countries (Basu, 2004).

Due to the poor productivity of the industrial sector coupled with the poor performance in other sectors, the whole economy was affected severely. The position became worsened in the beginning of the nineties when the financial position of the country deteriorated and was pushed to crisis. As a result of the borrowings from IMF India had to introduce its reforms and the objective of the reforms was to increase the economic efficiency of the system and this was sought to be achieved by the gradual removal of the barriers to entry and exit. The removal of such restrictions implied increased competition from firms entering with or without new technology and from foreign firms entering with new technology. After the reforms the firms have access to import of cheaper/better quality raw material, cheaper funds from abroad, ease of restructuring of the labour force and increased advertising expenditure. Earlier, the Indian firms had no access to the better quality or the cheaper raw material available outside the country and hence, they had to substitute inferior quality/expensive raw material, which implied a rise in the costs/poor quality of the goods produced. However, with the opening up of the economy the firms have full access to the foreign markets and could now use the better quality/cheaper raw material and therefore, could now cut down on the costs of the raw materials and hence, increase their efficiency. Secondly, due to the free access to the foreign markets the Indian firms can manage cheaper funds from abroad and thus, cutting down on the cost of using capital. Further, in the liberalized regime, to be efficient, firms are expected to restructure and to redefine the job responsibilities of the work force and thus, shed the excessive labour wherever needed. Also, since after the introduction of the reforms there is increased competition from multinational companies, which are known to enter on the basis of their brand names, the Indian firms are expected to increase their advertising expenditure in order to compete with their foreign counterparts. Also, the firms would be investing to strengthen their marketing and distribution channels.

Thus, in the light of the above arguments it is proposed to study the efficiency in the use of resources in the Indian manufacturing sector from 1990-91-2001-2002.

Section II Efficiency - Conceptual Issues

Looking at the development process of the economies over time, one may ask- 'why is it that people living in some economies experience high incomes, have access to more and better quality goods and on the other hand, there are economies in which people do not have access to as many goods as in other economies and even the quality of goods that they enjoy is far behind their counterparts?' 'Why is it that people living in one part of the world experience high growth rates while those living in the other parts experience low growth rates?' Although, undeniably there is more than one reason for this, the one argument that has attracted the collective attention of all the scholars is the efficient use of resources. Scholars have come to believe that in the context of the rising number of the people on earth and their equally rising aspirations coupled with the scarcity of the resources used in the process of production, it becomes imperative to use the resources at hand more efficiently. Since, the inefficiency in the use of resources is recognized as leading to substantial welfare loss (A.C. Harberger, 1959), it should not happen that the present generation consumes the maximum of the available resources and little is left to pass on to the future generations. The implications of this are quite stronger for countries that have been left behind in the process of development and have increasing number of people to feed and relatively lesser resources at their disposal. Initially, the economists concentrated rather over emphasized the role of capital and later, perhaps, as a reaction, focused more on the role of labour and population growth, the concept of the efficiency of resource use rarely received due attention. Whether it was Nurkse, who had suggested that the developing countries needed heavy doses of capital to move out of the vicious circle of poverty of low incomes and low savings, or it was Rodan who had stressed the need for developing incentives for investors to choose the right pattern of capital accumulation, efficiency in the use of all resources was never paid appropriate attention (I.J. Ahluwalia, 1991). Even Professor Rostow emphasized the need for a critical ratio of investment to national product as the right dose for moving from the 'take off' to 'sustained growth' and Arthur Lewis, similarly, suggested that the developing economies needed to save and invest 20 percent of its income (Thirlwal, 1989). Thus, the need for efficient use of the resources was nowhere to be seen in the picture. However, in the fifties the publication of studies by some eminent economists, unfolded the idea of achieving a high growth rate by cutting on the costs, which could be achieved by those economies as well that have been lagging behind in the process of development.

Meaning of Efficiency

Production is an act of converting inputs into output and in the process of production various resources/inputs are required. These inputs are capital, labour, raw materials and power and fuel. There is another important input that goes into the production of the goods i.e. the skills and the organisational capacity of the entrepreneur. Whenever there is a talk on the efficiency of the resources used in the production, it means the efficiency of all the above stated inputs. Before explaining the concept of efficiency it is crucial to know some of the issues attached to this concept. First, a nation can rarely be efficient as a whole. In a nation there will be sectors that are efficient users of resources and sectors which do not make efficient use of their resources. Even within an industry there will be firms that are efficient and that are not. Also, it is very rare that any single industry or a firm is efficient in all the areas. There might be areas where it is more efficient and areas where it is less efficient. We need to look at it in totality. Secondly, efficiency is related with existing competition and potential competition, which is reflected in the barriers to entry and exit. If there are internal and external barriers, there is every likelihood that inefficient firms are able to survive and it may also happen that at any time most of the firms in an industry are inefficient. Efficient use of resources would inevitably reflect in:

Unit or Average Cost of Production

Efficiency in terms of costs implies the production of goods at the minimum possible costs or alternatively it also implies that more goods are produced with the same resource cost. As a result of the reductions in costs there would be a downward shift in the costs curve signifying that the same level of output can be produced with lesser costs. The cost curve would shift from AA to BB.

Figure 1

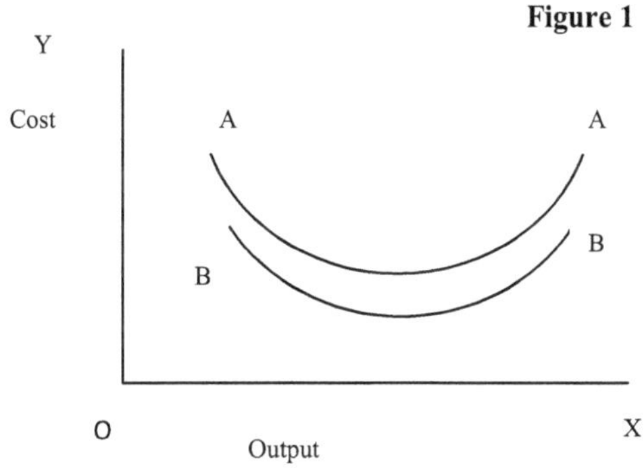

As a result this firm will experience expansion, which will benefit other firms through externalities in production. All those firms that supply it with raw materials, machinery, and other inputs would reap the economies of scale and will also reduce their costs. Ultimately, it will lead to a downward shift in the cost curves of the industry. If the quantum of this reduction in the costs is large then it will extend to other industries as well. At the macro level it will result in the general increase in the demand for goods and services so as to further stimulate the increases in the investment and thus, it will lead to an increase in the factor incomes thereby increasing the welfare of the people and hence, the consumer surplus. As a result there will be an improvement in the standard of living of the people as consumers, with the reduction in the prices, can now avail that bundle of commodities which was unattainable earlier.

Quality of Goods

Efficiency cannot be taken to mean the reduction in the costs alone. Many a time reduction in the costs and the quality of the goods goes hand in hand. For some time, it may happen that only the reduction in the costs is experienced and no improvement in the quality of the goods is being made. But in the long run both will be the feature of an efficient firm or of an industry. The production of poor quality goods in a competitive economy would lead to a virtual elimination of the firm from the market. With the reduction in the costs of an industry there will be an increased competition among the producers to sell their goods either by reducing prices or by improving the quality of their goods. Firms failing to do so appropriately and adequately would get eliminated in due course of time. This feature gets further support when it is viewed in the light of the multinationals. Multinational companies are known for the quality of their products and in this respect only those local firms would be able to survive that are efficient on both the counts.

Thus, efficiency in the resources used in the production can be explained through:

Production Function

The position of our industrial sector on the production function depends on how efficiently it is utilizing its resources. If the resources are underutilized then the position of the industrial sector will be somewhere under the production function (PP1) say at A (figure 2).

Figure 2

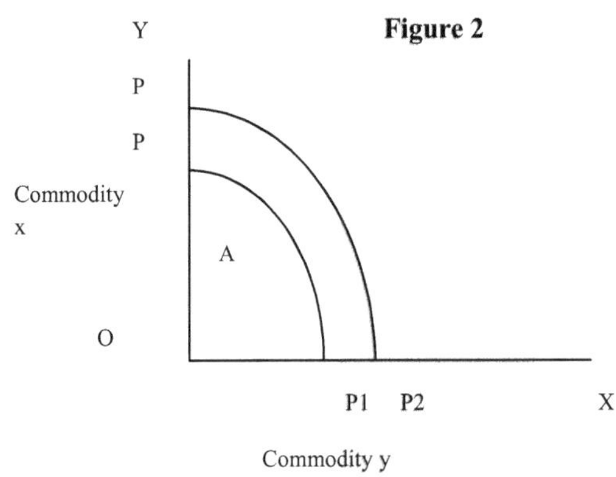

In this case the industrial sector is utilizing its resources inefficiently respective to its own production function and also in respect to the production function of the rest of the world i.e. PP2. The efficient use of the resources would lead to a change in the position of the economy i.e. from A to any point on its own production function.

Figure 3

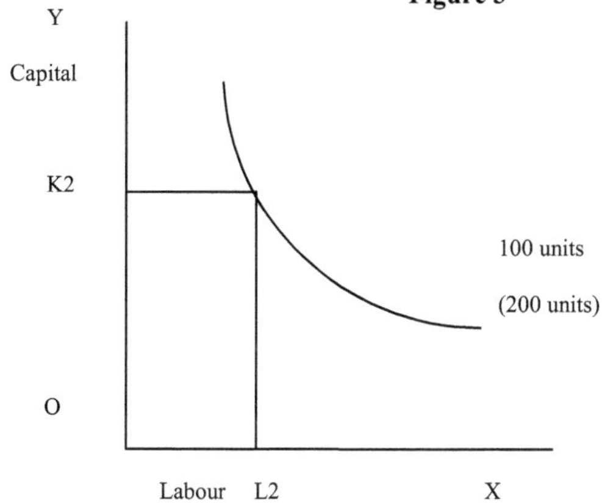

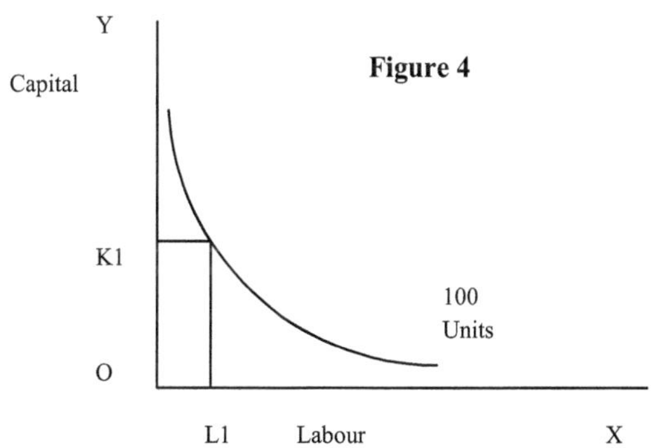

Figure 4

Isoquants

Efficient use of the resources implies that with the same resource cost a higher level of output can be produced. If earlier firm A was producing 100 units of output with a particular combination of capital (OK2) and labour (OL2) (figure 3) then by efficiently using its resources it can produce say, 200 units of output (same isoquant in figure 3 but with different output level) with the same combination of capital and labour signifying that the productivity of the factors has gone up. However, with output remaining the same if there is a reduction in the cost of the resources then, say, if earlier firm A was producing 100 units of output with a combination of OL2 units of labour and OK2 units of capital (figure 3) then with the efficient use of resources it would be producing the same output level with lesser quantities of inputs (OL1 units of labour and OK1 units of capital) as is evident from figure 4. Next, a detailed discussion on the efficiency of the various factors and how it can be measured is presented.

Efficiency in the Use of Capital

As has been mentioned earlier capital has received a lot of attention. The contribution of capital in the process of economic growth of the economies has been widely recognised. Ever since economics was established as a separate branch of study capital has been regarded as the central element in the production process. In fact economists have come to regard capital as the scarcest of all the scarce resources in the production process. However, the scarcity of the capital has made it indispensable that this factor of production should be efficiently used. Such an efficient use of capital becomes more acute in the context of the developing economies, which have relatively less capital at their disposal. But at the same time one faces a lot of problem in measuring capital. These are discussed below:

- **Problems In Defining Capital Employed**

There has been no consensus among economists on the issue of defining capital. In fact it is believed that- 'if economists reach an agreement on the theory of capital they will shortly reach agreement on everything else' (New Palgrave, 1987). Capital is to be distinguished from capital goods, which does not yield any immediate utility but produce goods that do so. Some define capital as an asset that yields an additional future stream of income to the society; however, such a definition would include all the consumption goods as capital.

Empirically, there are two concepts of capital that have come to forefront- a) capital is the discounted income flows derived from the asset. But there is no true measure of finding the expected future flow of such streams. b) The other way is to define it in terms of gross fixed assets as presented in the accounts of the firms but gross fixed assets may include historically valued assets, which does not give a true indication of the productive capacity of the capital. Usually, economists use Perpetual Inventory Accumulation Method (PLAM) to measure the amount of capital employed in production. In this method data is required on various variables like a time series of gross investment for each time period at current prices and a time series of price of capital goods and a 'measure' of depreciation. Moreover, one needs information on- that part of capital stock that is out of use between terminal year and the base year, identification of that part of capital stock which has experienced decline in its productivity, etc (Seth, 1999) and hence, one needs a measure of depreciation. But then one encounters the problem of choosing the right method for measuring depreciation, which is discussed in detail in the next part. Apart from this, while measuring the efficiency of capital through PLAM one encounters the problem of choosing the right price deflator.

- **Problems In Measuring Capital Consumed**

Whenever capital is employed and used overtime then some depreciation does occur. Depreciation is, thus, the decline in the value of the capital. This decline in the value of capital is the result of two factors- one, that its productivity may fall with use and two the expected future stream of incomes from that capital would be lesser as compared to the newer machines. Depreciation can be calculated by straight line method in which the cost of the asset minus the residual disposal value is divided by the number of years of its expected life to give the annual figure. But some scholars are of the opinion that the declining balance method should be used, which is a constant proportion of the value of the asset and hence, it is an annually diminishing amount. However, there are certain inherent limitations in this method that makes it a title tedious. Thus, there is no such measure that gives us true economic depreciation and whatever rules are there are just rules of thumb.

- **Capacity Utilisation**

Though the problems of defining and measuring capital have received great attention yet the problem of under utilisation or non utilization of the capacity of the plant has not received much attention. The concept of the utilization of the capacity assumes great importance in the context of developing economies like India where there is a great scarcity of capital. Moreover, the degree of capacity utilisation plays a vital role in the determination of the price cost margins among the industries (Sawhney and Sawhney, 1973). Capacity utilization is the ratio of the actual to the potential output. While the data for the actual output is easily available, the problem remains with the potential or the capacity output. In the traditional theory of the firm with U-shaped cost curves, the full capacity output is defined as the level of output associated with the lowest point on the average cost curve, thus, relating the concept of the capacity with the optimum utilisation of the resources. However, the concept of the U-shaped cost curves does not give room for the built in flexibility in the plants as it assumes that the plants are designed to produce only a unique and optimum level of output. Later on, when the L-shaped cost curves became popular, it became impossible to identify the exact minimum point on the LAC (Klein, 1960). However, with the development of the theory of duality, which suggested that there exists a cost function corresponding to the production function, it has become possible to estimate cost functions empirically but the supporters of the U-shaped cost curves criticize the empirical measure of the capacity output by duality as the data used is the accounting data and hence, the results are not reliable. Thus, the main issue is whether to define the capacity output in terms of the technical maximum (when the U-shaped cost curve after crossing the least cost point becomes vertical) or the economic maximum (at the least cost point) or in terms of the normal maximum (around the least cost point)? How to estimate it in relation to the working conditions: how many hours in a day, how many days in a year, how many shifts? (A Survey of Research In Economics - Industry, 1975). Also, there is a general tendency on the part of the reporting units to give wrong estimates of the capacity output particularly in the license raj period. The reason for this wrong reporting is that whenever these units wanted to get license for increasing their capacity they would give lower figures for the capacity output and higher for the production and whenever they wanted to restrict entry they would report the higher figures for the capacity and lower for the production. Thus, there are great problems in the measurement of the capital and capacity utilization.

Efficiency in the Use of Labour

Efficiency in the use of labour cannot be easily measured since labour is highly heterogeneous. There are differences in the labour at the level of the industry due to the differences in the educational qualifications of the labour force and differences in their skills. Even at the level of the firm there are differences in labour as even in a single firm, labour force with different skills are required. For example, in a firm there are workers with their different specializations and blue-collar employees with different specializations. Apart from the differences in the physical composition of the labour force there are differences in the quantum of mental and attitudinal effort of the labourers. There are huge variations in the differences in the perception levels of the labour force, which has a direct bearing on their efficiency. Two people with the same educational background and with the same job responsibilities may reflect differences in their efficiency due to their psychological, rational and intellectual differences. At the industry level these differences become more complicated and difficult to handle, as at this level the degree of these differences varies widely. Usually, economic theory makes the assumption of the homogeneous labour force. However, such an assumption does not do justice to the differences in the composition of the labour force and therefore, to their productivities. For the measurement of the efficiency of the labour force there is no such measure that covers the problem of the heterogeneity in full. 'Number of workers' does not take into account the contribution of the total employees of the firm (Goldar, 1986). 'Man days worked' is considered a better indicator of the efficiency of the workforce but one may ask that the mere presence of a person on his work does not imply that he is contributing positively to the firm. Wages and salaries is another important indicator of quantum of labour employed somewhat adjusted for the efficiency of the workers and of the employees. Precisely for this reason this indicator is used in this study. It is generally believed that the reduction in the wages and the salaries of a firm imply a reduction in labour costs, the reason for this reduction could be the shedding of the excessive labour force or due to their deliberate effort to restructure and cut down on costs. But this study does not cover the possible reasons for this reduction and therefore, their possible implications.

Efficiency in the Use of Raw Materials

Raw materials are an important contributor in the production of the goods. There is a whole lot of evidence that before the opening up of the economy there was a huge wastage in the use of raw materials. Thus, if under the open regime there is a cut in their wastage then it can be concluded that their efficiency has increased. However, per unit raw material costs depends on the prices of the raw materials as well. If there is an increase in their prices then this will lead to an increase in the costs of the raw materials per rupee of sales. But it cannot be concluded that the firm is inefficient since the efficiency in the use of raw materials depends on how it is used and rise in their prices is affected by a variety of factors. If effects of prices are adjusted by due deflator, decline in the raw material cost per rupee of sales is an appropriate indicator but this is not the only indicator of the efficiency of the use of raw materials. The composition of the raw material i.e. how much of it is imported from abroad since the imported raw material is known to be of cheaper and/or of better quality, also reflects its efficient use. Lastly, it may be that due to the lack of competition the producers use the locally available raw material whereas the better quality of raw material or the cheaper raw material was available elsewhere or in a different state. This could also be an important indicator of the efficient use of the raw materials.

Efficiency in the Use of Power and Fuel and Advertising Expenditure

Power and fuel is another significant input that goes in the production of goods. Indian firms are known to be very careless in the use of this particular input and hence, the result is the widening of the costs. But since with the pressures of competition, firms have a tendency to reduce their costs, reductions in the power and fuel/net sales indicates the efficient use of power and fuel by the firms. If the firms unable to sell the goods produced with the efficient use of resources then it has little meaning. Hence, advertising expenditure occupies an important place, particularly when the Indian firms face competition from MNCs, which are known to invest in brand building. If a firm is not investing in advertising then it may happen that the consumer is not even aware of that better quality product and hence, is buying the inferior quality product. However, if the firm increases advertising expenditure per rupee of sales and if its informative then the consumer would become aware of the better quality product and would prefer that over the inferior quality good and hence, his consumer surplus would increase and, on the other hand, with the rise in the demand for its product the firm will increase its production and hence, the firm will experience economies of scale and the producer would also be maximizing its surplus. Also, the final degree of efficiency is achieved when the firms go in for product differentiation. When competition increases advertising expenditure may be used as a proxy for product differentiation. Hence, a rise in advertising expenditure per rupee of sales means that the degree of product differentiation has increased. In this respect if a firm spends an increased amount on the advertising i.e. advertising costs/net sales increases then it indicates efficiency. Thus, efficiency is a broader concept than generally believed.

Economic literature reveals that there are studies that measure efficiency with the help of traditional measures (labour productivity, capital productivity) and there are studies that measure efficiency with the help of TFP. I.J. Ahluwalia's study done in 1991 is one of the most extensive and comprehensive studies. It analyses the long-term trends in the total factor productivity and partial factor productivities. This study covers the organised manufacturing sector of the Indian economy and ranges from 1959-60 to 1985-86. The analysis is undertaken at a very vast and extensive level as it includes the 63 two digit industry groups. It is also extended to the use-based sectors of the manufacturing. She uses the value added measure of output and applies the Growth Accounting Approach and the Production Function Approach. The total factor productivity growth is derived from the translog production function under the assumptions of competitive equilibrium and constant returns to scale. However, she also estimates alternative forms of the production function and also specifies the superiority of the translog production function. The data are obtained from Annual Survey of Industries. She uses wholesale price indices as deflators. Value added and capital stock is inclusive of depreciation and the capital stock is measured by the perpetual inventory accumulation method. For 1959-60 to 1985-86 the estimate of the TFP growth is (-) 0.4. Cotton textiles witnessed no growth and iron and steel and food products except for sugar registered a declining TFP growth. She also examines the long-term growth in the value added for the same period and it comes out to be 5.3 per cent per annum. The trends in labour productivity and capital productivity are quite striking, as the growth rate in the labour productivity was 2.2 per cent per annum and the capital productivity declined at the rate of 2.5 per cent per annum for 1959-60 to 1985-86. There was a decline in the labour productivity in sugar, non-ferrous metals and tyres and tubes. The other striking result is that the major contributor in labour productivity and in capital productivity is the consumer durables.

As per the use-based classification, intermediate goods experienced a growth of 4.8 percent in value added and (-) 1.2 per cent per annum in TFP, for the year 1959-60 to 1985-86. The growth in the value added and TFP in consumer non-durables was 4.5 and (-) 0.2 per cent per annum. However, the capital goods sector and the consumer durables performed better than their counterparts on both the counts. She further divides the study into four periods with a bit of overlapping in two periods. Period I consists of first half of the sixties, period II/III covers mid sixties to late seventies. Period IV covers the first half of the eighties. There was a decline in the growth in the value added from 9.1 in period I to 7.5 in period II. The figures for TFP are 0.2 for period I, (-) 0.2/ (-) 0.3 for period II and Ill and 3.4 in period IV suggesting improvements in the eighties. There was a decline in the capital labour ratios in the fourth period as well. In the fourth period i.e. in the first half of the eighties there was an increase in the labour productivity as compared to the first half of the sixties as the figure for manufacturing was 8.3 in period IV and 4.9 in period I. Similarly, in the case of capital productivity there was a marked improvement as the figure improved from (-) 3.8 in period I to 0.0 in period II. For the improvements in the eighties, the author gives credit to the changes introduced and the improvements in the infrastructure sector and in the agriculture sector. Lastly, she makes a comparison of India's productivity with the other developing economies and finds that India lags behind a number of countries like Argentina, Chile, Egypt, and Indonesia etc.

Sanjay Kathuria's (1995) study tries to explore the competitiveness of the Indian manufacturing industry. First, he explains the various factors that determine the competitiveness of any industry which are; exchange rates, unit labour costs and costs of the other inputs. He then explains the various measures of competitiveness: export propensity and market shares of the industries, and makes price comparisons of the goods produced by the Indian industries with the competing industries and lastly, he uses TFP for measuring the input efficiency. Export propensity is measured for the years 1973-74, 1978-79, 1987-88 and the ratios of manufactured exports to gross output were calculated from the study conducted by the World Bank in 1990. Out of the total sample of manufacturing industries (excluding gems and petroleum products) only non-metallic mineral products reported an increase in the export propensity signifying that the Indian manufacturing industries are highly uncompetitive. He then examines the price differences in India and the competing countries as this can give a broader and clear picture of the inefficiency. For this purpose, nominal protection coefficients (NPCs), which are the ratios of domestic prices to import prices, for the years 1986-87, 1988, 1989, were quoted from the same study. The results show that in all the manufacturing industries the (overall) NPC is greater than one, implying thereby that the prices prevailing in India are greater than the international prices, suggesting that the Indian goods are highly price uncompetitive. He then calculates the effective rate of protection (ERP), and domestic resource cost (DRC), for covering the problem of high taxes and tariffs. DRC measures the opportunity cost of earning or saving a unit of foreign exchange. The result shows that the Indian manufacturers are quite efficient but the reason for the low percentage of exports is the differences in the prices of the output due to the high input prices. The high input prices prevailing in the country in particular of the steel, other metals, plastics and oil products leads to high NPCs and thus, making the goods price uncompetitive.

For analysing the efficiency of the inputs used, he quotes the TFP growth for I959-60 to 1979-80, 1959-60 to 1965-66, 1965-66 to 1979-80, 1980-81 to 1988-89 from the study conducted by Ahluwalia and finds that between 1965-66 to 1979-80, there was a slowdown in the TFP growth in the value added, however, there was an upward trend in the eighties which coincides with the resurgence in the case of exports. He also points out that countries like Yugoslavia, Thailand and Indonesia have better TFP growth than India. Thus, his study finds that the manufactured products of India are price competitive if it is adjusted for price distortions but the share of its exports is very small. He finds that the reason for this distortion is the non-price factors like the government policy of restricting the internal competition and external competition, inhibiting the firms from attaining the optimal plant size, controlling the entry, exit and expansion of the firms, restricting the import of the technology and superior and cheaper raw materials. Lastly, he examines the firm level and the economy wide factors, like the characteristics of demand, affecting the competitiveness of the industry.

Further, S.L. Kansra and Rajeev Jain's (1999) study examines the response of the Indian corporate sector to an open and competitive environment due to the New Economic Policy. The study covers the 231 large private corporate firms for the years 1988-89,1989-90, 1990-91, 1991-92, 1992-93, 1993-94, 1994-95. The data is collected from CMIE. The study hypothesize that the industrial markets after the opening up of the economy are more contestable and competitive (both internally and externally) as before and thus, the firms are expected to respond by rationalizing the use of labour by redefining the job responsibilities, emphasizing on the training and shedding the excess labour, substituting the better quality and/or cheaper raw material from the foreign markets, cheaper funds from abroad, building their brand names by advertising and strengthening their marketing and distribution. The variables calculated are: net value-added per rupee of wage, average variable cost per rupee of sales, advertising, marketing and distribution expenditure per rupee of output, average variable cost and advertising expenditure per rupee of sales. These variables were calculated as averages for (1988-89, 1989-90 and 1990-91) and for 1991-92, 1992-93, 1993-94 and 1994-95 and difference of means test was employed. The results supported the hypothesis, as there was a significant increase in the net value added per rupee of wage and in the advertising, marketing and distribution per rupee of output and there was a significant decline in the variable cost per rupee of sales and in the variable cost plus advertising expenditure per rupee of sales. Thus, it signifies that the Indian firms have successfully reduced their input costs and are competing to their full with the foreign firms. Moreover, the study reveals that the greatest pressure of competition was on the producer goods firms and the consumer goods firms did not increase labour productivity but these firms are definitely working on strengthening their marketing, distribution and advertising. When the sample was divided into local and foreign firms it was found that the local firms experienced significant changes in all the variables where as in the case of foreign firms but for net value added per rupee of wage there was no significant improvement in any other variable. The local firms with no business house connections did not show any significant improvement in any of the variables.

S.L. Kansra (1999) undertakes a comprehensive study on the performance of the Indian corporate industries. The study, apart from analysing the efficiency in the resources, covers the R&D expenditure and it also compares the productivity comparisons of the various studies conducted by various authors. It categorizes the responses of the firms into three: the knee jerk response: cost reduction by the firms, increasing the advertising, marketing and distribution. Medium to long term response would be to upgrade technology through technical collaborations. Thus, this study covers both the short term and the long-term response of the firms. The variables are variable cost per rupee of sales, advertising, marketing and distribution expenditure/value of output, net value added per rupee of wage, R & D expenditure per rupee of sales. These variables are calculated for two periods (1988-89, 1989-90 and 1990-91) and (1991-92, 1992-93, 1993-94 and 1994-95) and difference of means test has been employed and sign test is also employed but with reference to R&D only. It covers 231 corporate firms and the data source is CMIE. The results are optimistic. In particular the response of the Indian corporate firms to the R&D intensity is positive and significant. The main highlight of the study is that if the 14 foreign firms are included in the sample of the local firms then the significant value of the R&D intensities disappears, signifying that the foreign firms depend on their parent companies for R&D. The results of the sign test support the hypothesis that the local firms are investing in R&D. Thus, this study gives an in depth analysis of the long-term and short-term response of the Indian corporate firms.

Unni Jeemol, N Lalitha and Uma Rani (2001) compare the growth and efficiency in the Indian organized and unorganized manufacturing with the growth and efficiency in the state of Gujarat, before and after the reforms. The study pertains to the period 1978-79, 1984-85, 1989-90 and 1994-95. For the unorganised sector the source of data is NSS and the CSO and for the organised manufacturing, data from ASI has been obtained. These data have been classified as per the user group classification. The TFP growth is taken as the difference between the growth rate in value added and a weighted sum of capital and labour growth rates. The deflators used in this study are the implicit deflators of GDP of the respective organised and unorganised manufacturing (two digit industry group). Total fixed asset have been used to represent capital and is deflated by the gross fixed capital formation given in the NAS. In order to deflate the gross value added and total fixed assets at the state level, the two digit industry group implicit deflators of gross domestic products and gross fixed capital formation for organised and unorganised manufacturing of the all India levels were used. For the all India levels the growth of the employment during 1978-95 was 1.3 percent in the organised manufacturing and 3.8 percent in the unorganised manufacturing. The growth in capital was higher in unorganised sector but the growth in value added was similar in both the sectors (at all India levels) but in Gujarat the growth in value added was higher than the all India figures and the trend in the growth in capital and labour in the organised and the unorganised sector of Gujarat was similar to the all India. The growth of TFP in the organised sector at the all India level was (-) 0.26, 4.00 and (-) 1.28, for 1978-85, 1985-90 and 1990-95 and for the unorganised it was (-) 14.57, 11.37 and (-) 3.13 for the same years. The figures for the unorganised sector of Gujarat was 0.39, 6.56 and 0.51 and for the organised sector of Gujarat was 0.76, (-) 9.45 and 7.36 for 1978-85, 1985-90 and 1990- 95. In the reforms period there was a decline in the labour productivity in the intermediate and consumer durables in the organised sector at the all India levels. For the same period a decline in the capital productivity was noticed in all the user groups in both the organised and unorganised sectors except for the consumer durables in the organised sector. Decline in the capital productivity was observed in all the user groups except for intermediate goods in organised sector for Gujarat. There was an increase in labour productivity in all the sectors of Gujarat except for capital goods and consumer non-durables. Thus, this study shows that the efficiency in the use of resources declined after the reforms.

Murali Patibandla and B V Phani (2002) focus on the factors that determine the micro level firm level productivity. It analyses the firm level productivity for the period 1989-99.The data were collected from CMIE. Productivity is measured on the basis of Farrel's Production Function. The industries covered are air conditioners, commercial vehicles, communication equipment, motorcycles, motor generators, pumps and compressors, refrigerators, tyres and washing machines. The variables are TFP, firm level exports plus imports of raw materials and capital goods/sales, imports of final goods/industry sales, Herfindhal index of degree of market concentration, degree of firm level vertical integration (value added/value of output), cumulative industry gross fixed assets to industry sales, MNC share of multinational firm's sales in total industry sales, research and development expenditure to sales. The strong result of this study is that there is significant and positive association between firm level productivity and a firm's outward orientation through exports and imports. However, the authors point out that any developing economy can realise the benefits of open and unrestrictive regime if there is government investment in higher and primary education and in research and development and steps should be taken to improve institutional conditions (informational perfections, reducing the market transactional costs).

Sumon Kumar Bhaumik and Subal C Kumhakar (2008) use plant level data to find if the post-reform growth is due to the efficient use of resources or larger use of factor inputs specifically capital. The study is from 1989-90 to 2000-01. The study finds that there was an increase in the productivity of factor inputs in 1990s but a larger part of the growth in the value added is explained by growth in the use of factor inputs.

Vinish Kathuria, Rajesh, S, N, Raj and Kunal Sen (2013) estimate the TFP growth of Indian manufacturing industries including formal and informal sectors. The study covers the period from 1994-95 to 2005-06. The authors use the three different techniques to estimate productivity. These are: growth accounting, production function accounting for endogeniety and stochastic production frontier. The authors conclude that the estimates of productivity for informal and formal sectors are different and the results are susceptible to the different techniques used.

Thus, there are more than one ways to measure efficiency.

Section III Methodology

The objectives of the present study are:

1. To examine whether there have been significant reductions in the components of the average variable cost in the post-reform period as compared to the pre-reform period.
2. To analyse whether there have been any significant increase in advertising expenditure of the firms in the post-reform period as compared to the pre-reform period.

For the pre-reform period data pertains to the years 1990-91, 1991-92, 1992-93 and for the reform period data pertains to the years 1999-2000, 2000-2001, 2001-2002. The year 1992-93 is included in the pre reform period because the economy was opened up in mid 1991 and the firms do take time to adjust to the changes and therefore, no immediate response is expected in the same year. However, in order to analyse the performance of the industrial sector in the middle years of 1990's, data for the years 1995-96, 1996-97, 1997-98 has also been covered. Difference of means test has been employed to test the significance or otherwise of the changes in the mean values of the variables. Therefore, a comparison of the average values of various variables for 1999-2000, 2000-2001, 2001-2002 (latter part of the decade of reform period) with average values of various variables for 1990-91, 1991-92, 1992-93 (pre reform period), average values of various variables for 1995-96, 1996-97, 1997-98 (mid of decade of reforms) with average values of various variables for 1990-91, 1991-92, 1992-93 (pre reform period) and average values of various variables for 1999-2000, 2000-2001, 2001- 2002 (latter part of the decade of reform period) with average values of various variables for 1995-96, 1996-97, 1997-98 (mid of decade of reforms). Since, the present study attempts to measure the efficiency of the variable factors, therefore, the efficiency of capital is not estimated in this study. The variables estimated in this study are given below:

1) Raw materials cost per rupee of sales (RMs/ Net sales)
2) Wages and salaries cost per rupee of sales (W&S/ Net sales)
3) Power and fuel cost per rupee of sales (P&F/ Net sales)
4) Advertising cost per rupee of sales (Adv/ Net sales)

The data for these variables have been obtained from CMIE. The sample selected by CMIE is based on the availability of the audited unabridged annual accounts of manufacturing companies. The industries covered include public sector companies (mostly Central Public Sector Enterprises), private sector, co-operatives and joint sector companies. It includes listed as well as unlisted companies. The latter are generally CPSUs and very large private limited Companies. The variables used in this study have been defined as (as per CMIE):

1) Sales

Income generated from main business activities like sale of goods and services, fiscal benefits, trading income. It also includes transfers but excludes expenses capitalised.

2) Net Sales

Sales excluding indirect taxes and duties such as excise, sales tax, octroi. Sales are also net of internal transfers.

3) Raw Material Expenses

Consumption of raw materials, stores as well as packaging expenses and purchase of finished goods for resale. Expenses incurred on inward transportation of raw materials form part of raw material expenses. Changes in the stock of semi-finished goods are netted off from the cost of raw material expenses.

4) Power and Fuel

This is the cost of energy like power, fuel, coal, etc.

5) Wages and Salaries

Includes payment made to employees such as wages, salaries, staff welfare, and allowances and perquisites. Director's remuneration forms part of wages and salaries. One time charge on account of YRS to revenue account is excluded from wages and salaries. However, deferred charge on account is included in it.

6) Advertising

This is the expenditure incurred on advertising.

Selection of Industries

CMIE takes only organised sector of the Indian manufacturing. Individual companies have been classified into the respective industry groups on the basis of homogeneous product groups contributing over 50 percent of the total sales of the particular companies. Wherever such clear-cut classification was not possible, the companies have been classified as 'diversified' units. The industries included in CMIE account for 70 percent of the organised industrial activity. Out of these industries 41 industries were selected and these account for 95.6 percent share in the sales of the total industries included in the CMIE. However, due to the low share in the value added of some of the industries, CMIE clubbed them together under one group as 'other food products', 'other textiles' etc. Since the share of these industries is very low it is not possible to deduce any statistical inference from such industries. Hence, such industries were not chosen for the analysis. The industries are:

1. Dairy Products
2. Tea and Coffee
3. Sugar
4. Vegetables Oils and Products
5. Beverages and Tobacco
6. Cotton Textiles
7. Synthetic Textiles
8. Inorganic Chemicals
9. Alkalies
10. Fertilizers
11. Pesticides
12. Paints and Varnishes
13. Dyes and Pigments
14. Drugs and Pharmaceuticals
15. Soaps and Detergents
16. Cosmetics and Toiletries
17. Organic Chemicals
18. Polymers
19. Plastic Products
20. Petroleum Products
21. Tyres and Tubes
22. Rubber and Rubber Products
23. Cement
24. Pig Iron and Sponge Iron
25. Steel
26. Ferro Alloys
27. Castings and Forgings
28. Metal Products
29. Non Ferrous Metals
30. Non Electrical Machinery

31. Electrical Machinery
32. Electronics
33. Transport Equipment
34. Automobile
35. Automobile Ancillaries
36. Paper and Paper Products
37. Leather Products
38. Books and Newspapers
39. Wood
40. Clocks and Watches
41. Diversified.

Any empirical study cannot be without inadequacies and when the study is on a topic like 'efficiency of resource use', there are bound to be some limitations due to the problems in defining various variables and their measures. This study is also not without flaws. In order to measure the efficiency in the use of capital Perpetual Inventory Accumulation method should have been applied which is a better indicator of the capital employed. Since, the present study covers the secondary data the Perpetual Inventory Accumulation method could not be applied. Decline in total wages given to the labour does not reflect declining efficiency. The decline in the total wages may have been due to the retrenchment of the labour. This study does not cover the loss of the employment caused by the reforms and therefore, does not cover the possible reasons for such a decline in the total wage bill or any social implication thereof. Apart from this the efficiency of the labour can also be judged by using the number of employees, the total man-hours worked instead of wages etc. and a direct comparison of the results of these indicators can be made but since CMIE does not give data on number of employees and on total man-hour worked, it could not be covered. Further, as is discussed earlier the efficiency in the use of raw materials is also reflected in the proportion of the raw material imported, which could be cheaper and/or of better quality as the higher the proportion of the imported raw material the greater the efficiency in the use of the same (assuming minimum wastage and any unnecessary rise in the prices which may disturb the cost of production). However, such data were not available. Secondly, in the pre reform period it may have been that the cheaper quality raw material or the better quality raw material was available elsewhere in the country but the producer preferred the local supplier and did not buy it from that part of the country. The reason for the same is the lack of internal competition. The other reason could be the various taxes levied by State governments restricting the supply of such raw material and the increasing transportation costs. Availability of the data on this measure could have revealed interesting facts but unfortunately CMIE does not provide data on this count.

In India there is perennial shortage of power and fuel. This is evidenced by the rising prices reflecting the pressure on the government to resort to apply the market prices. In such a case, if it is possible to find out that whether the industries are using their own power and how much or whether they are using power from GRID. Such an indicator could not be used due to the unavailability of the data. Availability of Kilowatt-hours of electricity used in generating a rupee worth of sales would have been the best but such data are not available. Also, a full-fledged study on the efficiency of resource use in the manufacturing sector should include the organised as well as the unorganised sector, ideally separately. However, the data of CMIE does not cover the unorganised sector. Hence, this study covers only the organised sector. Lastly, for estimating the true levels of efficiency, variables should have been deflated but in the pre reform period government used to regulate the input prices and these were deliberately kept low and the output prices were allowed to rise. Therefore, the differences in the output prices and in the input prices were very high. But in the post reform period government stepped back from the markets and the input prices are allowed to rise which does not lead to much of divergence between the two and hence, not much of difference in the prices of the inputs and output.

Thus, the concept of efficiency is a vast concept and a humble attempt is made in the next chapters to estimate it.

Chapter II

EFFICIENCY OF RESOURCE USE DURING PRE AND POST-REFORM PERIODS - A THEORETICAL DISCUSSION

The Indian industrial development can be briefly analysed under two heads - firstly under the controlled and the restrictive regime i.e. the pre reform industrial policy and secondly, under the open and less restrictive regime i.e. the post reform industrial policy. Firstly, the policies that were followed under the first regime, highlighting its salient features and its impact on the efficiency of the resource use are discussed and then the policies that have been followed after the 1991 and its postulated impact on the efficiency of resource use are explained. Following this the hypothesis is explained.

Section I Industrial Policy in the Pre Reform Period

The Indian planners were swayed by the idea of controlling the private initiative, private investment, markets, industry and guiding the growth and the direction of the economy for the betterment of all the sections of the society. This thinking was evident even in the pre independence period as the role of the state in the country's industrial development was discussed intensively among the dominant socio political leadership and the business class. The result of such discussions was the 'Bombay Plan', which argued in favour of the state interventions not merely to develop the physical and the social infrastructure but also to lead and guide the development of the private industrial sector (Degnbol-Martinussen, 2001). Although the signatories of the plan did not envisage a planned economy but what followed after independence i.e. the centralized planned economy, virtually controlled all the areas/sectors for diverting the resources and the initiative towards social good. Various factors like the inclination of the dominant political leadership of the day towards the socialistic pattern of growth, the success of the Soviet model of the centralized industrial development, the rejection of the market mechanism by majority of the economists and many other factors led to the adoption of a strategy in which 'state' was the leader (Kansra, 1999). This belief was further strengthened by the reports of the various committees like the report of the Monopolies Enquiry Commission (1964), the Mahalanobis report, and the report of the Dutt committee (1969). These reports conclusively proved that there was something rotten in the state of industrial administration (Eliot, 1971). Thus, the planners intended to build a system where all the sections of the society contribute to the development of the economy by placing the needs of the economy on top and their own needs on the bottom. For this purpose various restrictions were levied on the functioning of the private industrial sector in order to achieve the following objectives: to achieve self-reliance and to promote social justice

(Ahluwalia, 1991 and Srivastava, 1996). Self-reliance, as an objective, gained ground due to export pessimism and import substitution (the infant industry argument), which will be discussed in detail later. The social objective led to the creation of a wide and huge public sector and the support for the small-scale industries (which was finally changed to protection). And for the attainment of these two, the creation of the wide industrial base was indispensable. For realizing these objectives various kinds of policies and instruments were framed. These policies succeeded quite fairly as it led to the creation of the wide industrial base and the success of the import substitution policy increased our self-reliance. But the success was quite short lived as after the late sixties the industrial progress slackened down and thus, adversely affected the growth of the whole economy. Various studies revealed that in the course of achieving these objectives, such policies were framed that were unduly restrictive and led to the creation of an industrial sector that was not competitive, inefficient and under the pretext of protecting our industries, rampant oligopolies were created. Although some changes were introduced in the industrial policy in the eighties but it did not improve its performance significantly. Discussed below, is the detailed analysis of these policies that restricted competition and their impact on efficiency of resource use.

Policies that Restricted Internal Competition

Industrial policy resolution of 1948 was the first definite statement of the government towards industry. This resolution made it clear that both the public and the private sectors are going to play an important role in its development. This resolution reserved industries like the arms and ammunition, energy, railways and transport for the public sector and it was made clear that in the area of iron and steel, coal, ship-building etc, new establishments would be only by state. Apart from this there were industries that were reserved for government regulation like salt, tractors, automobiles, electricity etc. and the rest of the industries not included elsewhere were left for the private sector. Thus, this policy resolution laid the foundations for the concept of mixed economy. However, the Indian planners thought to regulate the working of the markets in order to steer clear the economy of concentration of the economic power in the hands of the few big business houses and this was sought to be achieved by the licensing system which came into being with the Industries (Development and the Regulation) Act of 1951. With this act it was made compulsory for the industries to obtain licenses to-

i) establish a new undertaking,

ii) for manufacturing a new article in an existing undertaking,
iii) expanding capacity,
iv) producing a good that was later brought under licensing,
v) for changing a location (Desai, 1988).

The government thought that the best way to rule out the concentration of the economic power was to restrict and regulate the internal competition i.e. the virtual elimination of the 'contestability' of the markets (Bhagwati, 1993). Meanwhile, the First Five Year Plan was framed and implemented and the results were so strongly positive that it made the planners and the leaders to believe that the policy that they had decided for the country was the best policy and it needed to be strengthened with more instruments that could lead to a faster realization of the objectives. With this aim in mind the Industrial Policy Resolution of 1956 was announced that gave a new classification of the industries and the industries were divided into three schedules. In Schedule A as many as 17 industries were reserved for the public sector and Schedule B covered those industries that were to be gradually state owned and the number of industries was 12. Remaining industries were left in Schedule C which were left for the private sector but it was mentioned very clearly that these industries were also to be controlled (Bandyopadhyay, 2009). Thus, this policy virtually enabled the government to widen its jaws over the markets by widening the area to be under its direct control and thus, giving more than the desirable role to the public sector. With this resolution it became apparent that there was going to be a huge expansion of the public sector and it was going to be the leader in the growth of the country and the private sector was only going to play the role of the younger brother. With in no time public sector expanded rapidly from infrastructure to the basic and heavy industries, from power generation to chemical industries, from tourism to bread manufacture. Public sector was to be seen everywhere. The industries that were reserved for the private sector were regularly controlled by several acts like the Essential Commodities Act (1955). With this act wider powers were conferred on to the government to control the production, supply, distribution of the items declared as essential. Controls were exercised over iron and steel, coal, fertilizers, and cotton textiles. These controls were motivated by the desire to ensure allocation of adequate amounts to 'priority' sectors often at some reasonable price (for example the control over iron and steel, cement), some were motivated by the equity considerations (like motor cars), and the other reason was to prevent the inflationary effects. But the failure of such a policy was apparent as the priorities were not clearly defined and allocations were not made as per the objectives of the policy. Moreover, it so happened that the public sector commodities were sold to the private sector at lower costs whereas, no or little control was exercised on the private sector to sell their commodities, made with the help of the public sector good, at lower prices. As a result the producers of the public sector good were deprived of huge profits that meant loss of revenue to the government and the final consumer was also deprived of the benefits of the controlled prices (Bhagwati and Desai, 1970). With the emphasis of the large-scale sector on the capital-intensive techniques, to help create greater employment opportunities the small-scale sector was promoted to foster the growth of industries with the labour intensive techniques and to aid in the spread of industrialization to the rural and backward areas. However, with the passage of time the policy of promoting these industries changed to protecting these industries. With the industrial licensing policy of 1977 and 1980, these industries received further support in the shape of various concessions and protection from the large-scale industries.

Apart from the above stated barriers there were additional barriers to the growth and diversification of larger firms. The Monopolies and Restrictive Trade Practices Act (MRTP), 1970 was introduced with the aim of preventing the concentration of economic power and to prohibit such monopolistic activities that may have adverse effects on public interest. Under this act the firms were declared as MRTP firms whose assets were more than Rs 1 billon or more and the dominant firm was declared as the one whose assets ranged above Rs 10 million. These firms were not allowed to enter the new areas without taking the permission of the authorities and even within their area of operation these firms were not allowed to expand their capacity without taking clearances from the authorities. As a consequence the firms were not allowed to gain the required size that could make them internationally competitive (Goswami and Mohan, 1996). In addition to controlling the growth of the national industries, the level of foreign investment in domestic industry was also to be controlled, and the domestic industries were to be restrained from making technical collaborations with the foreign firms in order to protect the domestic industries and to save the scarce foreign exchange. To meet this end, Foreign Exchange Regulation Act was passed in 1973 that allowed only a maximum of 40 percent equity by any foreign firm and the permission of the RBI was also required for the same. Restrictions were also imposed on the non-residents on their holding up of assets in India and on Indians on holding up of assets abroad. Barriers to take-overs were also imposed in order to support the above stated control.

The Companies Law put restrictions on the acquisitions and mergers and transfer of shares and hence, it prevented effective entrepreneurship.

In addition to the barriers to entry there were barriers to exit as well. The labour laws were stringent and rigid. In order to protect the interests of the labour class, BIFR was set up which made it mandatory for the firms intending to shut down to take the prior approval of the board. Thus, a loss making company was not allowed to shut down, as it would lead to the loss of employment; for example in 1985 there were 120000 'sick' units of which only 60 closed down that year (Srivastava, 1996). Even the redeployment of the workers, within plants or to other locations, was severely resisted. Section 25(N) of the Industrial Disputes Act, 1947 provides that, no workman employed in any industrial establishment to which Chapter V (B) applies, and who has been in continuous service for at least one year (or 240 days) in that establishment can be retrenched without, a) being given three months notice in writing indicating reasons for retrenchment; and b) the period of the notice having expired; and c) prior permission being sought from the appropriate government agency in a prescribed manner. Further, an order of the appropriate government or in the specified authority granting or refusing to grant permission, shall be final and binding on all parties concerned, and shall remain in force for one year from the date of such order. Thus, the retrenching of the labour force required prior approval and in most of the cases such decisions were given in the favour of the labour class (Goswami and Mohan, 1996). Such a policy led to the over protection of the workers in the organised sector as compared to the workers in the unorganised sector. Such over protection led to the unnecessary burden on the public sector companies and also on the private sector companies.

Policies That Restricted External Competition

In order to protect the infant industries from external competition, various kinds of restrictions were imposed on the free import and export of the goods, capital, and technology and knowhow. For this purpose Import Control Act (1947) was framed that provided for obtaining licenses for the import of various kinds of goods. These licenses were classified into many categories and the two main categories were the 'actual user' (AU) licenses for the import of intermediaries and raw materials and capital goods (CG) licenses for the import of capital goods. These licenses were non transferable and were allocated either on the basis of the 'essentiality' of the imported item or on the basis of the 'indigenous unavailability' of the proposed good to be imported. Thus, the allocation of the licenses depended upon the decision of the bureaucrats. Later on, under the open general license the import of certain types of the raw materials, intermediate goods and the capital goods were allowed but these were subjected to various types of tariffs (Srivastava, 1996). The tariff structure in India was highly complex which sometimes led to a single commodity often attracting multiple tariff rates (Goswami and Mohan, 1996). According to the World Bank, in November 1989, the basic customs duties ranged from 0 percent to 355 percent and auxiliary duties from 0 percent to 45 percent while countervailing duties ranged from 0 percent to 50 percent (Siggel, 2001).

In respect to exports there was this strong belief of export pessimism among the developing countries and India was no exception to that. Prebisch and Singer postulated that since the developing countries exported agricultural goods, the terms of trade were bound to go against these countries and in the favour of developed countries that exported the industrial goods. Engel also said that the income elasticity of demand of food products has a tendency to be less than one and those of the industrial goods is more than one. Thus, these studies popularised that the developing countries, owing to the composition of their exports, are on a losing side. As a result in the case of the exports the planners chose to be pessimistic. Exports were also subject to licensing as per the import-export policy. These categories were- items not allowed, items allowed on merits, items restricted to quotas etc. (Siggel, 2001) and thus, the restrictions on exports led to a slow and slackened growth of the economy. However, other developing nations adjusted their trade policies with time and took advantage (for example Korean manufactured exports that were negligible in 1962 increased to nearly four times that of India's exports in 1980 {Bhagwati, 1993}), the Indian planners remained stuck to their export pessimism. Various other types of programs like the Phased Manufacturing Programs and the Industrial Regulatory Reform System were also followed that controlled Indian companies from buying goods from abroad. Whatever incentives for exports were available, were not strong enough to improve the exports of the manufacturing firms (Raut, 2002-03). Thus, the Indian trade policy restricted the outward orientation and in the name of inward orientation the policy of import substitution was promoted and lead to the substitution of the poor quality and relatively expensive goods to the better quality and the cheaper goods available from abroad. Also, the import of the capital and of technology by the Indian firms was restricted causing a huge difference in the efficiency of the firms in India as compared with the industrially developed nations and also with other developing countries.

Such restrictive policies as were being followed in the sixties slowed down the growth of the economy through causing a fall in the productivity levels despite the fact that India achieved a very high rate of savings. This slow down in the productivity level was supported by various studies; the TFP growth was (-) 1.8 as per the study done by Mehta for the years 1959-70, (-) 0.2 as per the study done by Brahmananda (1950-80) and Ahluwalia's estimates were (-) 0.6 and (-) 0.2 for the years 1959-79 and 1959-86 respectively (Kansra, 1999). Bhagwati points out three reasons for this lackluster performance: a) excessive bureaucratic controls over production, investment and trade, b) inward looking trade and foreign investment policies and c) a substantial public sector. Such policies clearly eliminate internal and external competition and therefore, question the objectives of the planners to achieve the goal of reducing monopoly power. Also, the unwarranted growth of the public sector with reduced contribution to the state's exchequer became a drain on the resources of the economy. As a result of the inefficiency of the public sector, coupled with the restrictions on the growth and diversification of private sector the whole of the industrial sector witnessed a huge decline in the efficiency of the resources used. The end result was that the Indian industry remained well below the potential production possibility frontier both with reference to the domestic PPF and to the PPF of the rest of the world. The impact on the efficiency of the resources is discussed in detail below:

Creation of an Industrial Sector with Oligopolies

With full protection to the industries from external competition and the presence of the internal barriers to entry and mobility of the firms created enough conditions for the creation of oligopolies which were confirmed by various studies like Gupta (1968), Ghosh (1975), Sawhney and Sawhney (1973). Bhagwati and Desai (1970) sums up the whole argument of the encouraging oligopolies as,

'The first major point that comes to an economist, when discussing the question of monopoly and competition in the Indian economy, is that a very large segment of the economy ... works under monopolistic conditions. The creation of new capacity in the organized industrial sector is strictly controlled at various levels. Capital issues control, licensing and the permission to import machinery are the principal points at which the entry into the industry is controlled by the government. The net effect of this system is that the entry by the new firms is completely ruled out, as the government will not allow creation of more capacity than current and estimated demand. It thus, rules out the elimination of the inefficient producers by the efficient ones. It also rules out the possibility of the more efficient, current units expanding and eliminating the inefficient current units: expansion by the current units is as much subject to control within targets as expansion through new firms. If, then, the competition from efficient rivals at home is ruled out by our economic planners, what about foreign competition? Here again competition has no chance.'

Creation of Sub Optimal Capacities

Indian firms were always restrained from obtaining the optimal plant size (Kansra, 1990). This was due to the limitations imposed by the authorities on capacity and expansion and the encouragement of the entry of the small firms. For example, in major industries such as steel, cars, light commercial vehicles, chemicals, aluminium, paper, average plant sizes were small relative to the international norms (Kathuria, 1995). As a result of these sub optimal capacities, the average costs of these firms were high as a result of which their goods had to be priced high and the consumers had no choice but to buy these goods (of poor quality due to no competition) at high prices and thus, suffer a loss in the consumer surplus.

Diversified Structure and Specialization

For achieving the goal of self-reliance Indian industrial policy encouraged the setting up of a wide industrial base. As a result, there was huge diversification of the industries. Many firms produced some or most of the inputs themselves that led to high costs but since there was no competition, the rising cost was ignored. The difficulties in the availability of the raw materials particularly in the eighties and the lack of specialization encouraged the firms to take their (raw materials) production in their own units or units under their control. Restrictions on the expansion of big business houses forced them to take licenses for even unrelated products contributing in diversifying the industrial structure (Kathuria, 1995). Throughout this policy, the cut in the rising costs was always pushed in the background due to the lack of competition.

Loss in Consumer surplus and Producer Surplus

Due to the creation of an oligopolistic structure, the customers were used to the idea of standing in the long queues or waiting for 4-5 months to get the product. Even the 'controlled' items were black marketed and thus, it deprived the original consumer of the benefits of the reduced prices leading to a loss in the consumer surplus and the objective of social justice was never achieved rather the opposite happened. The undue restrictions on the firms led to the 'shortages' of the inputs and it resulted in the rising prices of the inputs and thus, it led to the rise in the cost of production of the firms across the board to other firms in the whole industry, though the impact varied from case to case depending on the degree of backward and forward linkages. Thus, the rise in the costs percolated to all most all the firms and it did not allow the producers to maximize their surplus.

Non-Availability of the Better Quality or Cheap Raw Material

The restrictions on the imports meant complete unavailability or the restricted quantities of the imported raw material (even in the case of the restricted quantities the tariffs were so high that they were made costlier), which was known to be of better quality and /or cheaper, implied the substitution of the poor quality or expensive raw material or the firms were encouraged to take up their in-house production. As the requirements were generally small, the sub optimal production was mostly at high costs and hence, there was a rise in the total unit cost of production and/or the poor quality goods were supplied. Even within the country if better quality or cheaper raw material was available in a different state, the producers preferred to buy it locally because high costs could be passed on to the consumers, as there was little competition. Such behaviour inevitably led to the inefficient use of resources.

High Power and Fuel Costs

Since the majority of the industrial sector was under the government, including the production of power and fuel, there emerged a culture within the public sector units to use these resources freely and the wastage of power and fuel was a regular feature, implying huge power and fuel costs. Even with-in the private sector units high power and fuel costs were a regular feature due to the lack of stress on the efficient use of resources.

Capacity Utilization

The low capacity utilization was a prominent feature of the industrial sector in the pre reform period, which implied the inefficient use of capital in a capital scarce country. Various studies demonstrated that the capacity utilization figures were very low. The figure for the capacity utilization was lowest in the capital goods sector in the 1970's, which was the centre of India's industry. The capacity utilization ratios for the capital goods sector were 66.4 percent, 60.2 percent, 59.4 percent, 67.3 percent and 62.4 percent in 1966-67, 1976, and 1977 respectively (Ahluwalia, 1991).

Technology

The policy of restrictions on the import of technology and know - how or the foreign collaborations prevented the industries to make use of the superior technology available outside and substitute their needs with the locally available outdated and inefficient technology. However, when such a policy is followed it is expected that the government expenditure on Research and Development would rise significantly at least in the initial years when the private sector would not be motivated to invest in R&D. However, this did not happen. The expenditure of the government on R&D was not sufficient to meet the needs of the growing industrial sector and the private sector investment, as expected in the initial years, was also low in R&D. The total expenditure (government and non government) on the Research and Development as percent of sales on applied research as a percent of GDP was 0.4 percent against 1 .65 percent, 1.56 percent, 1 .83 percent, 2.03 percent of USA, U.K., Japan, and Germany respectively (Kansra, 1999).

Entrepreneurship

Kathuria argues that due to the existence of the excessive restrictions on entry, exit and mobility and a variety of constraints on the use of resources and techniques, the Indian entrepreneur would spend their valuable time and money to retain lobbyists so as to grab the licenses. Also, the absence of competition and of motivation among the entrepreneurs led to the attitude of using the age-old processes and thus, would not make use of their own skills or would not make any or little effort to acquire new skills. The instability in the policies and the high levels of direct and indirect taxation were also responsible for the lack of interest on the part of entrepreneurs. Thus, the rigid and restrictive policy framework was responsible for the poor efficiency of the resource use. The efficiency of the firms was low in comparison to the other firms in the industry and in comparison to the firms in the foreign countries. The poor productivity of the industrial sector coupled with the poor performance in other sectors, affected the whole economy severely (Kathuria, 1995).

Section II Industrial Policy after the Introduction of the Reforms

In the early 1980s with the publications of the various studies, which reflected the poor productivity growth, there was an increasing realization among the economists, policy makers, the industrial and the business class people, that the system of control and restrictions on the growth of the industrial sector was largely responsible for the derailing of the development process of the economy. As a result various policy measures were announced in the eighties that were meant to loosen the controls and the restrictions. However, with the weakening of the political leadership at the union and the state level, and the simultaneous emergence of the regional parties marked the beginning of competition among the political parties for votes implying increased, unnecessary, irrational and uneconomical favours (for example increased amount of subsidies) that ultimately increased the borrowings of the government and thus, weakened its financial position (Degnbol-Martinussen, 2001). Nayyar sums up these changes in the 1980s as, 'First, there was a proliferation of subsidies. Some, such as the subsidies on food, fertilizers and exports, were explicit. These meant unnecessary increase in expenditure. Others were implicit in under-priced services of public utilities such as irrigation, electricity and road transport, or in under-priced goods produced in public sector such as steel and coal. These meant revenue foregone (Nayyar, 1998).'

Thus, the perusal of a policy that promoted the existence of wide spread inefficiencies in public as well as in the private sector ultimately pushed India to the economic crisis of 1990, when the levels of inflation and fiscal deficit increased alarmingly and the foreign exchange reserves dipped an all time low. As a result of the crisis, India had to borrow money from IMF and had to agree to open up its economy. Thus, the New Economic Policy was introduced in India with a view to redefine the role of the public sector, expanding it in some areas and reducing in other areas, and of the private sector. The New Economic Policy stated,

"After the initial exuberance of the public sector entering new areas of industrial and technical competence, a number of problems have begun to manifest themselves in many of the public enterprises. Serious problems are observed in the insufficient growth in productivity, poor project-management, over-manning, and lack of continuous technological up-gradation and inadequate attention to R&D and human resource development. In addition, public enterprises have shown a very low rate of return on the capital invested. This has inhibited their ability to regenerate themselves in terms of new investments as well as in technology development. The result is that many of the public enterprises have become a burden rather than being an asset to the government. The original concept of the public sector has also undergone a considerable dilution."(Chandra and Chandra, 1997).

The objective of the reforms was to improve the economic efficiency of the system in terms of resource allocation or use. And the instruments to achieve this were the gradual removal of the barriers to entry and the restrictions on growth of firms (Rangarajan, 2001-02). In July 1991, government announced a number of changes in the industrial, foreign trade and in the area of foreign investment. Industrial licensing system was abolished and roughly 80 percent of the industrial sector was freed from the system of licensing. Licensing was required for only a few industries. These were: coal and lignite, petroleum, sugar, animal fats and oils, cigars and cigarettes etc. Specific reforms were introduced to increase private sector participation and to achieve this, the industries reserved exclusively for the public sector were reduced to 18. These were:

- Arms and Ammunition and allied items of defense equipment, defense aircraft and warship.
- Atomic Energy.
- Coal and Lignite.
- Mineral Oils
- Mining of iron ore, manganese ore, chrome ore, gypsum, sulphur, gold and diamond.
- Mining of copper, lead, zinc, tin, molybdenum and wolfram.
- Minerals specified in the schedule to Atomic Energy (Control of production and use) Order 1953.
- Railway Transport (Kapila, 2001-02).

The government also decided to disinvest its stake in various PSUs. And to end the various procedural delays, all the registration schemes were abolished and the entrepreneurs were required to file an information memorandum on new projects and expansions (Gupta, 2000). The New Economic Policy also saw a change in the attitude of the government towards foreign investment and technology as it was realized that the foreign competition in the domestic markets will pressurize the local producers to cut down on their costs and to produce goods of international quality and the added advantage would be the inflow of the modern technology. As a result the foreign direct investment was allowed up to 51 percent in high priority industries. There was a considerable removal of the procedural delays in order to attract the foreign investors. The import of components, raw materials and intermediate goods and payment of know - how fees and royalties were also smoothened (Palande, 2000). In case of the foreign technology, automatic permission was allowed in high priority industries up to a lump sum of Rs. 1 crore. MRTP was replaced by Competitions Act in 2002, which was amended in 2007 and FERA was replaced by FEMA in 1999, in order to allow Indian firms to gain considerable size and compete with foreign firms in India and to allow them to invest in the foreign economies. Import duties were also reduced in stages and the controls on exports were also reduced. Thus, the majority of the sectors were opened up after 1991 though in various stages. Due to the reform measures and the competition from the foreign companies there has been an upward movement in the efficiency levels of the Indian industrial sector. But the reform process slowed down after the initial years of 1990s and there was a marked slowdown in the industry after 1997-98, which affected the performance of the manufacturing industries. Though the performance of the industrial sector has been inconsistent but the service sector has been able to push the growth rates. With the increase in investment in infrastructure sector by the government and the rise in the construction sector has generated employment opportunities. However, industrial sector even after the introduction of reforms has failed to give consistent growth and employment. Many believe that the non-implementation or the slow implementation of the announced measures and the strategy of the government to take no or little steps to remove the barriers to exit are affecting the efficiency levels (Gokarn, 2001). However, the postulated impact of the reforms on the efficiency level is discussed in detail in the next section.

Postulated Impact on the Efficiency of Resource Use

The opening up of the economy implied dismantling of the various barriers to entry and barriers to mobility and thus, there is increased competition from firms entering from different industries with or without new technology, and from foreign firms entering with new technology. Due to the changes done in MRTP and FERA the firms are allowed to grow large and the indigenous firms are investing in foreign economies. Joint Ventures with the foreign firms are taking place. Under such a competitive environment the Indian firms are expected to cut down on their wasteful expenditure and thus, reduce their costs and make better use of capital, shedding of the extra labour and the increase in the productivities of all the inputs. Since the MNCs are known for their quality products there should be an increased attempt on the part of the Indian companies to improve the quality of their products. With the import restrictions cutting down the Indian firms are substituting the better quality and the cheaper raw material for the earlier used costly and/or poor quality raw material. There should be an increased tendency on the part of the producers to cut down the unnecessary use of power and fuel and to hire power from the cheapest source. The MNCs are known for their brand building and to face these challenges the Indian firms should be obliged to increase their advertising expenditure and strengthen their marketing and distribution channels, which leads to product diversification. All this should increase the efficiency of the Indian firms.

As per the Global Competitiveness Report, 2015 (World Economic Forum), India has moved up sixteen places to rank 55th out of 140 economies on a global index of competitive economies. This is largely due to the improvement in the competitiveness of country's institutions, its macroeconomic environment and better infrastructure (The Economic Times, September 30, 2015). However, it is not to be forgotten that in 2003-2004, India was at 56th position out of 102 economies. Thus, current achievement reflects the slowdown. But all this apart, the economists fear that the delays on the part of the government to implement various reform measures and in particular the reforms relating to the barriers to exit may affect the industry adversely (Kabra, 2002).

Section III Hypothesis

Based on the above arguments, it is expected that the Indian firms would be importing cheaper raw materials, better quality raw materials; firms would be economizing on the use of raw materials; there would be restructuring of the labour force, downsizing the employment where needed, redefining the job responsibilities; firms would manage cheaper funds from abroad; there would be an increase in advertisement expenditure to confront MNCs. Thus, the following hypothesis would be tested in the study: the efficiency of resource use in the Indian industries in the post reform period is likely to increase. Hence, the firms would be

- Reducing the various components of the average variable cost i.e. there would be a significant reductions in:
  a) Raw material cost/net sales (RMs/Net sales),
  b) Wages and salaries cost /net sales (W&S/Net sales), and
  c) Power and fuel cost/net sales (P&F/Net sales).
- An increase in the product differentiation is expected which is reflected in:
  a) The increase in advertising expenditure cost /net sales (Adv/Net sales).

On the basis of the above stated hypothesis, the performance of the Indian industries would be analysed from 1990-91 to 2001-2002. The empirical analysis is presented in the next chapter.

Chapter III

EFFICIENCY OF RESOURCE USE DURING PRE AND POST-REFORM PERIODS - AN EMPIRICAL DISCUSSION

Section I Industry-wise Analysis

Using resources efficiently has been identified as the key factor for the brisk growth of any economy. As it has been mentioned earlier, initially, economists did not lay stress on the efficient use of all the inputs. In the pre reform period the stress was on meeting the physical targets rather than on the efficient use of resources. It has been lately recognised as the prime force for the faster growth of the industrial sector of any economy. Since the under developed and the developing countries are short of resources and have growing population to demand more and more resources, it is imperative to know whether these scarce resources have been used efficiently or not and thus, has any difference been made to the development of the industrial sector and to the rest of the economy through the efficient use of resources or not.

In this chapter it would be explored whether the efficiency in the use of resources has improved after the introduction of reforms that signifies a more open and a more competitive regime. For this purpose 41 industries have been covered. Efficiency has been sought to be measured by calculating a) raw materials cost per rupee of sales b) wages and salaries cost per rupee of sales, c) power and fuel cost per rupee of sales, d) advertising cost per rupee of sales. These ratios have been calculated for the years (1990-91, 1991-92, 1992-93), and (1995-96, 1996-97, 1997-98), and (1999-2000, 2000-2001, 2001-2002). Difference of means test has been employed to test the significance or otherwise of the changes in the Mean values of the variables. Financial ratios for each industry are given in Appendix 1. Based on the assumption that there is not much of divergence in the input prices and in the output prices after the introduction of reforms, a few things about the efficiency of the variables are discussed below:

- Before the reforms, prices of fuel and power were deliberately kept low. Government would rarely increase their prices. However, after the introduction of the reforms, with the increased stress on the less interference of the government, prices were bound to increase and thus, the prices of fuel and of power were increased. So, if there is an increase in power and fuel cost/net sales then it is does not imply inefficiency (because of the rise in their prices). If the ratios have gone down then it is definitely indicative of the rise in the efficiency levels, as despite the rise in the prices there has been an effort in the concerned industry to cut down on its costs.

- Since prices are assumed to not to diverge, increase in raw material cost/net sales implies a fall in the efficiency levels of the industry and decrease in these variables implies that the resource has been efficiently used.
- As we mentioned earlier this study does not cover the loss in the employment caused by the reforms. If there is an increase in the wages and salaries cost per rupee of sales in a particular industry then it might be that the productivity of the workers/employees has improved and as a result their wages and salaries have been increased in the industry. In the decade of the introduction of reforms it is expected the firms to redeploy and restructure their workers and staff, which is bound to affect their productivity and their remuneration.

Industry wise results are presented below:

Manufacture of Dairy Products

The Indian dairy products industry has an overwhelming large part in organized and in the informal and unorganised sector. The latter part is highly competitive; however, the organized sector has had a very low degree of competition from domestic, as well as producers from abroad for a very long period of time. It was only in the latter part of the 1990's that controls over the domestic and foreign entry of the dairy products was relaxed a bit but still the degree of foreign competition is quite low. The response of the industry is given in table 3.1 (all the tables are given at the end of the chapter). As we can see from the table the following variables have declined significantly: raw material costs/net sales (in 1999-02-1990-93 and in 1999-02-1995-98) and power and fuel cost/net sales (in 1999-02-1990-93 and in 1995-98-1990-93). As we said earlier in the beginning of the same chapter there is bound to be a rise in the prices of the power and fuel after the introduction of the reforms and if any industry is able to cut down on its costs per rupee of sales then it is indicative of the efforts that the industry has put in to cut down these costs. Raw material costs/net sales were also significantly reduced. Hence, these two resources have been efficiently used in this industry. The following variables were noticed to be increasing significantly: wages and salaries cost/net sales (in 1999-02-1990-93 and in 1999-02-1995-98) and advertising cost/net sales (it was significant in 1999-02-1995-98). Rise in the wages and salaries per rupee of sales, as mentioned earlier, might be because that the productivity of the workers and staff has increased and as a result there has been an increase in the wages and salaries in order to boost the morale of the workers. Rise in advertising costs/net sales indicates that the industry is preparing itself well to face competition from the multinational companies, which are known to sell their goods on the base of their brand names. Thus, rise in the cost of advertising per rupee of sales implies efficiency.

Manufacture of Tea and Coffee

Response of tea and coffee industry is given in table 3.2. The table shows that a significant fall was observed in raw material costs/net sales. Thus, this industry has been using raw materials efficiently. Significant rise was observed in the following variables: wages and salaries cost/net sales (in 1999-02-1990-93 and in 1999-02-1995-98), power and fuel cost/net sales (in 1999-02-1990-93 and in 1999-02-1995-98) and advertising cost/net sales (in 1999-02-1990-93). Thus, this industry is also spending heavily to sell its goods through advertising, which is indicative of the rise in the efficiency. Rise in wages and salaries per rupee of sales might be due to the increased payments on account of the rise in productivity. And the rise in power and fuel costs per rupee of sales cannot be interpreted as inefficiency as their prices have been rising after the introduction of the reforms. Thus, on the whole this industry can be said to be utilising its resources efficiently.

Manufacture of Sugar

Table 3.3 shows that there was a significant reduction in the following two variables: wages and salaries cost/net sales (in 1995-98-1990-93) and power and fuel cost/net sales (in 1999-02-1990-93 and in 1995-98-1990-93). No significant change was noticed in rest of the variables. Thus, this industry is also using its resources efficiently. But this industry is not spending on advertising, which might be because it faces very little competition from foreign companies.

Manufacture of Vegetable oils and Products

The results of this industry are presented in table 3.4. The data presented in the table explains that there have been significant reductions in the following variables: wages and salaries cost/net sales (in 1999-02-1990-93 and in 1995-98-1990-93) and power and fuel cost/net sales (in 1999-02-1990-93). Also, there has been a significant rise in the following two variables: raw material cost/net sales (in 1999-02-1990-93 and in 1995-98-1990-93) and advertising cost/net sales (in 1999-02-1990-93). Vegetable oils and Products seem to be struggling a bit to cut down on the costs of raw material per rupee of sales but on the whole their performance and their response to the challenges of liberalization has been very positive.

Manufacture of Beverages and Tobacco

Ever since the Indian economy is opened up, beverages and tobacco have faced full competition. Table 3.5 shows that raw material cost/net sales fell significantly after the introduction of reforms. This rise was uniformly experienced in all the three periods (1999-02-1990-93, 1995-98-1990-93 and 1999-02-1995-98). Therefore, beverages and tobacco industry used raw materials efficiently. Power and fuel cost/net sales fell significantly in 1995-98-1990-93 but again rose significantly in 1999-02-1995-98. There was a significant rise in advertising cost/net sales in 1999-02-1990-93 and in 1995-98-1990-93 but in the 1999-02-1995-98 there was a significant decline in this variable. And thus, apart from the consistent decline in the raw material cost per rupee of sales, most of the variables have shown inconsistent performance. This industry cannot be termed as efficient.

Manufacture of Cotton Textiles

It is evident from table 3.6 that there has been a significant decline in: wages and salaries cost/net sales (in 1999-02-1990-93 and in 1995-98-1990-93). However, significant rise was experienced in: advertising cost/net sales (in 1999-02-1990-93 and in 1995-98-1990-93) and power and fuel cost/net sales (in 1999-02-1995-98). Thus, this industry has also used its resources efficiently, as there was a decline in the cost of wages and salaries per rupee of sales and a rise in advertising costs per rupee of sales. Rise in power and fuel cost /net sales could be traced to the rise in their prices.

Manufacture of Synthetic Textiles

Synthetic textiles have been responding inefficiently to the calls of competition after the introduction of the reforms, as table 3.7 reveals, there was a significant rise in: power and fuel cost/net sales (in 1999-02-1990-93). A significant fall was experienced in advertising cost/net sales in 1999-02- 1990-93 and in 1995-98-1990-93. Therefore, there has been inefficient use of the resources in this industry.

Manufacture of Inorganic Chemicals

Data in the table 3.8 depicts the response of Inorganic Chemicals industry. The table highlights that there has been a significant fall in: raw material cost/net sales (in 1999-02-1990-93). There was a significant rise in: wages and salaries cost/net sales (in 1999-02-1990-93), power and fuel cost/net sales (in 1999-02-1990-93 and in 1999-02-1995-98) and advertising cost/net sales (in 1995-98-1990-93). As mentioned in the beginning of the present chapter, rise in wages and salaries cost per rupee of sales could be indicative of the rise in productivity and the rise in advertising cost per rupee of sales shows that this industry has been investing in building its brand name. On the whole this industry has been responding as per the hypothesis.

Manufacture of Alkalies

Response of Alkalies industry has been very poor. As is evident from table 3.9, significant rise was noticed in: raw material costs/net sales (in 1999-02-1990-93 and in 1999-02-1995-98), wages and salaries cost/net sales (in 1999-02-1990-93 and in 1995-98-1990-93) and power and fuel cost/net sales (in 1999-02-1990-93). No rise was noticed in the advertising cost/net sales. As a result of the rise in the cost of most of the variables it can be concluded that this industry is not using its resources efficiently.

Manufacture of Fertilizers

Fertilizer industry has again been using its resources inefficiently. Table 3.10 shows that there was a significant rise in wages and salaries cost/net sales in 1999-02- 1990-93 and in 1995-98-1990-93. There was no significant change in rest of the variables. This industry did not make any contribution to increase the advertising cost per rupee of sales.

Manufacture of Pesticides

As is evident from the data in table 3.11, there have been some significant changes in this industry since the introduction of reforms. There was a significant decline in wages and salaries cost/net sales in 1999-02-1990-93 and in 1995-98-1990-93. Advertising cost/net sales also increased significantly in 1999-02-1990-93 and in 1995-98-1990-93. There was a rise in power and fuel cost/net sales in 1999-02-1990-93 but in 1995-98-1990-93, it declined significantly and in the next period there was a significant rise in the same variable, which depicts inconsistent response. Despite the inconsistency in the response of power and fuel cost/net sales it can be said that this industry has responded well.

Manufacture of Paints and Varnishes

The response of this industry is given in table 3.12. As the table reveals there have been some significant declines in: raw material cost/net sales (in 1999-02-1990-93 and in 1999-02-1995-98), power and fuel cost/net sales (in 1999-02-1990-93 and in 1999-02-1995-98), advertising cost/net sales (in 1999-02-1990-93, 1995-98-1990-93 and in 1999-02-1995-98). Though, the significant decline in the first two variables indicates efficient use of the two resources, the decline in advertising costs per rupee of sales is contrary to the hypothesis. But in totality this industry can be termed as efficient.

Manufacture of Dyes and Pigments

Dyes and pigments industry responded significantly and positively (table 3.13) in wages and salaries cost/net sales (in 1999-02-1995-98), advertising cost/net sales (in 1999-02-1990-93, 1995-98-1990-93). Significant fall was noticed in raw material cost per rupee of sales in 1999-02-1995-98. Rise in advertising costs per rupee of sales and the fall in raw material costs per rupee of sales has been as per the hypothesis.

Manufacture of Drugs and Pharmaceuticals

Drugs and pharmaceuticals industry's response is given in table 3.14. The table shows that there were significant reductions in: wages and salaries cost/net sales (in 1999-02-1990-93 and in 1995-98-1990-9) and power and fuel cost/net sales (in 1995-98-1990-93). Thus, the response of this industry has been as per the hypothesis and hence, it has been using its resources efficiently.

Manufacture of Soaps and Detergents

As we can see from table 3.15 there was a significant rise in power and fuel cost/net sales in 1999-02-1990-93 and in 1999-02-1995-98 but this does not imply that this resource has been utilized inefficiently. Soaps and detergents industry has not made any significant increase in advertising cost per rupee of sales and being a consumer industry, which is open to full competition from foreign companies, it is imperative for this industry to spend on advertising and reach out to consumers before its foreign competitors, which are known to woo their customers on the basis of their brands. Also, no significant contributions were made to cut down on raw material costs per rupee of sales and wages and salaries cost per rupee of sales. Hence, this industry has been inefficient in the use of the resources.

Manufacture of Cosmetics and Toiletries

As revealed from the data presented in table 3.16 the following variables were found to be declining significantly: raw material cost/net sales (it declined in 1999-02-1990-93 and in 1995-98- 1990-93, however, in 1999-02-1995-98, it increased significantly). The following variables increased significantly: wages and salaries cost/net sales (it increased significantly in 1995-98-1990-93 but in 1999-02-1995-98 it declined significantly), power and fuel cost/net sales (significant increase was experienced in 1999-02-1990-93 and in 1995-98-1990-93 but in 1999-02-1995-98, it declined significantly) and advertising cost/net sales (in 1999-02-1990-93 and in 1995-98-1990-93). Although there was a significant rise in wages and salaries cost/net sales and in power and fuel cost/net sales in the initial years yet the subsequent fall in latter part of the reforms shows the efficient use of the resources. The rise in raw material cost per rupee of sales in the latter part is against the hypothesis but the rise in advertising cost per rupee of sales implies the stress of the industry to spend on building their brand names.

Manufacture of Organic Chemicals

Organic chemicals response is given in table 3.17. There was a significant rise in the following variables: raw material cost/net sales (it increased in 1995-98-1990-93), power and fuel cost/net sales (in 1999-02-1995-98). Significant decline was noticed in advertising cost/net sales in 1999-02-1990-93. Its response cannot be termed as positive and therefore, it can be said that this industry has not utilized its resources efficiently.

Manufacture of Polymers

Table 3.18 shows the response of this industry. Significant rise was noticed in the following variables: raw material cost/net sales (in 1999-02-1990-93) and wages and salaries cost/net sales (in 1995-98-1990-93). No significant change was noticed in the rest of the variables. Polymers industry is not utilizing its resources efficiently.

Manufacture of Plastic Products

The response of this industry shows that this industry is cutting down on raw material costs per rupee of sales. As table 3.19 shows, there was a significant decline in raw material cost/net sales (it declined in 1999-02-1990-93 and in 1999-02-1995- 98). Significant rise was noticed in wages and salaries cost/net sales (in 1999-02-1995-98) and power and fuel cost/net sales (in 1999-02-1990-93 and in 1999-02-1995-98). As indicated earlier in the present chapter the rise in power and fuel costs per rupee of sales couldn't be interpreted in terms of inefficiency, therefore, it can be said that the plastic products industry is using its resources efficiently.

Manufacture of Petroleum

Petroleum industry is quite efficient in the use of resources. Table 3.20 reveals that there was a significant rise in: raw material cost/net sales (in 1999-02-1990-93 and in 1999-02-1995-98), power and fuel cost/net sales (it increased in 1999-02-1990-93 but declined in 1995-98-1990-93, rose again in 1999-02-1995-98) and advertising cost/net sales (in 1999-02-1990-93). Since the rise in the power and fuel cost per rupee of sales cannot be interpreted in terms of the rise in inefficiency levels, thus, it can be said that this industry has been utilizing its resources efficiently.

Manufacture of Tyres and Tubes

The response of the tyres and tubes industry is given in table 3.21. As is evident from the table there has been a significant rise in: wages and salaries cost/net sales (in 1999-02-1990-93 and in 1999-02-1995- 98) and power and fuel cost/net sales (in 1999-02-1990-93 and in 1999-02-1995-98). Raw material cost/net sales declined significantly in 1999-02-1990-93. There was no significant rise in advertising cost/net sales. Hence, the tyre and tubes industry has been utilising its resources inefficiently.

Manufacture of Rubber and Rubber Products

Rubber and rubber products industry has responded very well to the liberalized regime. Table 3.22 shows that there has been a significant fall in raw material cost/net sales in 1999-02-1990-93. Significant rise was noticed in: power and fuel cost/net sales (in 1999-02- 1995-98) and advertising cost/net sales (in 1999-02-1990-93). Rise in the advertising cost/net sales and cut in the raw material cost/net sales has been as per our hypothesis. Thus, rubber and rubber products industry has been responding positively by utilizing its resources efficiently.

Manufacture of Cement

The response of the cement industry is given in table 3.23. There has been significant rise in: power and fuel cost/net sales (in 1995-98-1990-93) and advertising cost/net sales (in 1995-98-1990-93). No significant reductions were made in raw material cost/net sales and in wages and salaries cost/net sales. The response of this industry has been below average and hence, this industry has been utilising its resources inefficiently.

Manufacture of Pig Iron and Sponge Iron

Table 3.24 shows significant rise in: raw material cost/net sales (in 1995-98-1990-93) and wages and salaries cost/net sales (in 1999-02-1990-93 and in 1999-02-1995- 98). Power and fuel cost/net sales declined significantly in 1999-02-1995-98. Despite the rise in the prices of power and fuel this industry has managed to cut down its costs. The rise in the wages and salaries per rupee of sales can be due to redeployment or restructuring of the labour force. But this industry could not control the rise in the raw material costs and hence, this industry has utilised its resources inefficiently after the introduction of the reforms.

Manufacture of Steel

As is evident from table 3.25 steel industry seems to be going through its bad phase in the 1990's as a number of variables responded opposite to the hypothesis. Significant rise was noticed in the following variables: raw material cost/net sales (in 1999-02-1990-93 and in 1995-98-1990-93), wages and salaries cost/net sales (in 1999-02-1995-98) and power and fuel cost/net sales (in 1999-02-1990-93). Advertising cost/net sales declined significantly in 1999-02-1990-93. Thus, this industry seems to be suffering hard in order to cut down on costs after the introduction of reforms.

Manufacture of Ferro Alloys

Table 3.26, shows that this industry did not respond to more liberalized regime, as there were no significant changes in the variables in any of the periods covered. Hence, its efficiency has neither improved nor deteriorated.

Manufacture of Castings and Forgings

Castings and forgings industry responded as per the hypothesis. Table 3.27 shows that the following variables declined significantly: wages and salaries cost/net sales (in 1999-02-1990-93 and in 1995-98-1990-93), power and fuel cost/net sales (in 1995-98-1990-93). There were significant increases in: raw material cost/net sales (it increased significantly in 1999-02-1990-93 and in 1995-98-1990-93 but it declined in 1999-02-1995-98) and advertising cost/net sales (in 1999-02-1990-93). Thus, this industry has efficiently used its resources. The rising raw material cost per rupee of sales was also checked in the latter part of the decade of the introduction of reforms and there were significant reductions in wages and salaries costs per rupee of sales and in power and fuel costs per rupee of sales. Hence, the response of this industry has been as per the hypothesis.

Manufacture of Metal Products

Metal industry has definitely improved its performance as per the needs of the open and competitive regime. Table 3.28 reveals that there have been significant reductions in: raw material cost/net sales (in 1999-02-1990-93 and in 1995-98-1990-93) and wages and salaries cost/net sales (in 1999-02-1990-93 and in 1999-02-1995-98). Significant rise was experienced in: power and fuel cost/net sales (in 1999-02-1990-93 and in 1999-02-1995-98) and advertising cost/net sales (in 1999-02-1990-93). As we have mentioned earlier in the present chapter the rise in power and fuel cost per rupee of sales cannot be termed as the rise in the efficiency levels of the concerned industry. Hence, the metal products industry is utilising its resources very efficiently as there are significant reductions in the raw material costs per rupee of sales and in wages and salaries cost per rupee of sales and in order to compete with MNCs it has also increased its advertising cost per rupee of sales.

Manufacture of Non Ferrous Metals

Table 3.29 elucidates the response of this industry in the various periods. As is evident from the table there were significant reductions in three variables. These variables are: wages and salaries cost/net sales (in 1999-02-1990-93), power and fuel cost/net sales (in 1999-02- 1990-93) and advertising cost/net sales (in 1999-02-1995-98). Raw material cost/net sales increased significantly in 1999-02-1990-93 and in 1995-98-1990-93. This industry has responded totally opposite to the hypothesis related to advertising. Its response was to reduce the advertising cost per rupee of sales. However, the reductions in the wages and salaries cost per rupee of sales and in power and fuel cost per rupee of sales is commendable and hence, it can be said that this industry's response is as per the hypothesis.

Manufacture of Non-Electrical Machinery

Non-electrical machinery's response is given in table 3.30. Advertising cost/net sales did not show any signs of improvement in any of the periods. Wages and salaries cost/net sales also did not show any significant reductions. However, raw material cost/net sales did decline significantly in 1999-02-1990-93 and in 1995-98-1990-93. Power and fuel cost/net sales increased significantly in all the three periods. Hence, the response of non-electrical machinery can be said to be as per the hypothesis and is using its resources efficiently.

Manufacture of Electrical Machinery

Electrical Machinery has responded very well after the opening up of the economy. Table 3.31 shows significant reductions in wages and salaries cost/net sales in 1999-02-1990-93 and in 1995-98-1990-93. Advertising/net sales increased significantly in 1999-02-1990-93 and in 1995-98-1990-93. There were no significant changes in the rest of the variables. Hence, the efficiency in the use of resources of the electrical machinery has increased after the opening up of the economy.

Manufacture of Electronics

Electronics industry is open to full competition from foreign firms. It is expected that this industry will respond positively by utilising its resources efficiently so as to compete with the foreign competitors. Table 3.32 reveals that there were significant reductions in: raw material cost/net sales (in 1999-02-1990-93 and in 1999-02-1995-98) and power and fuel cost/net sales (in 1999-02-1990-93 and in 1999-02-1995-98). Significant rise was experienced in: wages and salaries cost/net sales (in 1999-02-1995-98), advertising cost/net sales (it increased significantly in 1995-98-1990-93 but it declined in 1999-02-1995-98). The reductions in raw material cost/net sales and in power and fuel cost/net sales have been as per the hypothesis but the significant rise in wages and salaries cost/net sales and the fall in advertising cost/net sales in the latter part of the decade of the introduction of reforms goes against the hypothesis. However, as mentioned in the beginning, there is a need to look at the efficiency of an industry in totality, as it is very rare that an industry is efficient in all the areas simultaneously. Thus, it can be said that this industry has utilised it resources efficiently.

Manufacture of Transport equipment

Table 3.33 shows that there were significant reductions in: wages and salaries cost/net sales (in 1999-02-1990-93 and in 1995-98-1990-93). Significant rise was noticed in: power and fuel cost/net sales (in 1995-98- 1990-93) and advertising cost/net sales (in 1999-02-1990-93 and in 1999-02-1995-98). Thus, it can be concluded that this industry is utilising its resources efficiently, as the response of the variables was as per the hypothesis.

Manufacture of Automobile

Automobile industry faces full internal and external competition. As is evident from table 3.34 this industry responded only to the changes in advertising cost/net sales as the value for advertising/net sales was significant in all the three periods. There were no significant changes in the rest of the variables. This industry did not respond by cutting down on wasteful costs but it significantly increased its advertising expenditure. On the whole, it can be said to be marginally efficient user of the resources.

Manufacture of Automobile Ancilliaries

Automobile ancillaries industry's response is given in table 3.35. There were significant reductions in wages and salaries cost/net sales in 1999-02-1990-93. And power and fuel cost/net sales increased significantly in 1999-02-1990-93 and in 1995-98-1990-93. Since the rise in power and fuel cost/net sales cannot be interpreted as inefficient, so it can be said that this industry is utilising the resources efficiently.

Manufacture of Paper and Paper Products

Table 3.36 reveals that this industry is utilising its resources inefficiently as there was a significant rise in raw material cost/net sales in 1999-02-1990-93, in 1995-98-1990-93, and also in 1999-02-1995-98. There were no significant changes in the rest of the variables. Thus, the response of this industry has been contrary to the hypothesis.

Manufacture of Leather Products

Leather Products industry showed no significant change in any of the variables in any of the periods as is given in table 3.37. Thus, this industry did not respond to the changed regime in the 1990's.

Manufacture of Books and News Papers

Books and Newspaper industry has responded very sharply and very positively in the liberalized period. Its response has been as per the hypothesis. Data in table 3.38 reveals that there was a significant cut in wages and salaries cost/net sales in 1999-02-1990-93. Significant rise was experienced in: power and fuel cost/net sales (in 1999-02-1990-93 and in 1999-02-1995-98) and advertising cost/net sales (in 1999-02-1990-93). The rise in power and fuel cost/net sales can be ignored and hence, it can be said that the efficiency in the use of resources, in this industry, has increased after the introduction of reforms.

Manufacture of Wood

Table 3.39 presents the response of this industry. This table shows that there were significant increases in the following three variables: wages and salaries cost/net sales (in 1999-02-1990-93 and in 1999-02-1995-98 but in 1995-98-1990-93 the value declined significantly), power and fuel cost/net sales (in 1999-02-1990-93 and in 1999-02-1995-98) and advertising cost/net sales (in 1999-02-1990-93 and in 1995-98-1990-93). As is evident from the response, this industry has been underperforming, as it is unable to utilise its resources efficiently after the introduction of reforms.

Manufacture of Clocks and Watches

Clocks and Watches face full competition. Its response is given in table 3.40. Wages and salaries cost/net sales increased significantly in 1999-02- 1990-93 and in 1995-98-1990-93. Power and fuel cost/net sales were significantly reduced in 1999-02-1990-93 and in 1995-98-1990-93 but the same were increased significantly in 1999-02-1995-98. No significant changes were made in advertising cost/net sales and raw material cost/net sales. The performance of clocks and watches has been a mixed bag. The reductions in power and fuel cost/net sales have been a good sign but the same were significantly positive in the latter part of the decade of reforms. On the other hand, the rise in wages and salaries cost/net sales can be because of the rise in the productivity levels and the increased remunerations to them. Hence, it can be said that this industry has been utilizing its resources efficiently.

Manufacture of Diversified

The responses are given in table 3.41. As is evident from the table wages and salaries cost/net sales were significantly reduced in all the three periods. Advertising cost/net sales increased significantly in 1999-02-1990-93. Thus, this industry has also responded as per the hypothesis and has been utilising its resources efficiently.

Section II Conclusion

Considering that it is very rare that an industry is efficient in all the areas simultaneously, it can be said that the response of the majority of the manufacturing sector has been as per the hypothesis. Two industries did not respond significantly to the open and liberalized regime. These industries were Ferro Alloys and Leather Products. Twenty-seven industries responded as per the hypothesis to the emerging competitive threat. These were:

- Dairy Products,
- Tea and Coffee,
- Sugar,
- Vegetable oils and Products,
- Beverages and Tobacco,
- Cotton Textiles,
- Inorganic Chemicals,
- Pesticides,
- Dyes and Pigments,
- Paints and Varnishes,
- Rubber and Rubber Products,
- Drugs and Pharmaceuticals,
- Cosmetics and Toiletries,
- Plastic Products,
- Petroleum,
- Castings and Forgings,
- Metal Products,
- Non Ferrous Metals,
- Electrical Machinery,
- Non Electrical Machinery,
- Electronics,
- Transport Equipment,

- Automobile,
- Automobile Ancilliaries,
- Books and Newspapers,
- Clocks and Watches, and
- Diversified.

Out of the total 41 industries 12 industries did not respond to the emerging competition as per the hypothesis. These industries were:

- Synthetic Textiles,
- Alkalies,
- Fertilizers,
- Organic Chemicals,
- Polymers,
- Tyres and Tubes,
- Soaps and Detergents,
- Paper and Paper Products,
- Cement,
- Pig Iron and Sponge Iron,
- Steel, and
- Wood.

However, the performance of the industries can also be compared across the board i.e. the number of industries that have been able to cut down raw materials cost/net sales, wages and salaries cost/net sales, power and fuel cost/net sales and increase the advertising costs/net sales.

Raw Material Costs/Net Sales

Only 12 industries could significantly reduce raw material costs/net sales. These were: Dairy products, Tea and Coffee, Beverages and Tobacco, Inorganic Chemicals, Paints and Varnishes, Dyes and Pigments, Plastic Products, Rubber and Rubber Products, Metal Products, Non-Electrical Machinery, Electronics, and, Tyres and Tubes. But 9 industries experienced the rising share of raw material costs per rupee of sales and these industries were- Vegetable Oils and Products, Alkalies, Organic Chemicals, Petroleum, Pig Iron and Sponge Iron, Steel, Non-Ferrous Metals, Paper and Paper Products, Polymers. Eighteen industries did not respond significantly (Sugar, Cotton Textiles, Synthetic Textiles, Fertilizers, Pesticides, Drugs and Pharmaceuticals, Soaps and Detergents, Cement, Ferro Alloys, Electrical Machinery, Transport Equipment, Automobiles, Automobile Ancilliaries, Leather Products, Books and Newspapers, Clocks and Watches, Wood and Diversified) and 2 industries displayed inconsistency in their performance (Castings and Forgings, Cosmetics and Toiletries).

Power and Fuel Costs/Net Sales

Eighteen industries were found to be experiencing the trend of rising power and fuel/net sales. These industries were: Tea and Coffee, Cotton Textiles, Synthetic Textiles, Inorganic Chemicals, Soaps and Detergents, Organic Chemicals, Plastic Products, Tyres and Tubes, Steel, Non-Electrical Machinery, Alkalies, Rubber and Rubber Products, Cement, Metal Products, Transport Equipment, Automobile Ancilliaries, Books and Newspapers, Wood. But as explained earlier in the present chapter there were bound to be rise in prices of the power and fuel during the reform period, hence, the rise in power and fuel/net sales cannot be termed as rise in the inefficiency levels. On the other hand, only 9 industries could cut down power and fuel costs per rupee of sales. These industries were: Dairy Products, Sugar, Vegetable Oils and Products, Paints and Varnishes, Drugs and Pharmaceuticals, Castings and Forgings, Non-Ferrous Metals, Electronics, Pig Iron and Sponge Iron. The cut in the power and fuel/net sales is definitely indicative of the efficient use of the resource concerned. The rest of the industries either did not respond (Fertilizers, Dyes and Pigments, Polymers, Ferro Alloys, Electrical Machinery, Paper and Paper Products, Automobiles, Leather Products, Diversified) or their response was not consistent (Beverages and Tobacco, Pesticides, Cosmetic and Toiletries, Petroleum Products, Clocks and Watches).

Wages and Salaries Cost/Net Sales

Thirteen industries experienced significant reductions in wages and salaries/net sales. These were: Sugar, Vegetable Oils and products, Cotton Textiles, Pesticides, Drugs and Pharmaceuticals, Castings and Forgings, Metal Products, Non Ferrous Metals, Electrical Machinery, Transport Equipment, Automobile Ancillaries, Books and Newspapers, Diversified. However, 14 industries experienced rise in this variable. These were - Dairy Products, Tea and Coffee, Beverages and Tobacco, Inorganic Chemicals, Alkalies,

Fertilizers, Dyes and Pigments, Polymers, Tyres and Tubes, Plastic Products, Pig Iron and Sponge Iron, Steel, Electronics, Clocks and Watches. This rise in wages and salaries cost/net sales may tentatively be taken to indicate rising labour productivity. Twelve industries did not respond significantly. These were- Synthetic Textiles, Paints and Varnishes, Cement, Ferro Alloys, Non Electrical Machinery, Organic Chemicals, Soaps and Detergents, Paper and Paper Products, Leather Products, Automobiles, Rubber and Rubber Products, Petroleum. The response of Cosmetics and Toiletries industry was inconsistent.

Advertising Cost/Net Sales

Industries displayed good performance in the case of costs of advertising per rupee of sales, as 19 industries had increased their expenditure on advertising per rupee of sales. Industries included in this category were- Dairy Products, Tea and Coffee, Vegetable Oils and Products, Cotton Textiles, Inorganic Chemicals, Pesticides, Dyes and Pigments, Cosmetics and Toiletries, Petroleum, Rubber and Rubber Products, Cement, Castings, and Forgings, Metal Products, Electrical Machinery, Transport Equipment, Automobile, Books and Newspapers, Wood and Diversified. Only 5 industries (Synthetic Textiles, Paints and Varnishes, Organic Chemicals, Steel and Non- Ferrous Metals) cut their advertising costs per rupee of sales and 15 industries did not respond (Sugar, Alkalies, Fertilizers, Drugs and Pharmaceuticals, Soaps and Detergents, Polymers, Plastic Products, Tyre and Tubes, Pig Iron and Sponge Iron, Ferro Alloys, Non-Electrical Machinery, Automobile Ancilliaries, Paper and Paper products, Leather Products and Clocks and Watches). Beverages and Tobacco and Electronics did not show consistent performance.

As explained earlier that the variables could not be deflated due to the reasons highlighted earlier, the significant rise in the components of average variable cost could not be interpreted as the rise in the inefficiency levels. But the significant fall in these variables is definitely indicative of the rise in the efficiency in the use of resources. And since the present study is focusing on the performance of the industries in totality, so in this respect it can be concluded that despite the rise in the costs of power and fuel per rupee of sales significant efforts have been made to reduce the share of raw material costs per rupee of sales and costs of wages and salaries per rupee of sales and as mentioned earlier, it is very rare that a particular sector is efficient in all the areas simultaneously, as a whole and also it is very rare that with in that sector a particular industry is efficient in all the areas simultaneously, and also, within the same industry there can be firms that are efficient and those that are not efficient. Based on these lines it can be said that the Indian manufacturing sector has definitely improved its performance after the introduction of the reforms as 27 industries responded as per the hypothesis and hence, the efficiency in the use of resources has improved. And since some reforms particularly related to barriers to exit are yet to be implemented, a further rise in the efficiency of the resources used in the process of production is expected. The industries that are struggling should concentrate on the efficiency of the resources used in the process of production otherwise when the degree of competition is going to be increased then these industries would be wiped out of the market. The studies done in this area have also concluded that there has been a definite improvement in the efficiency of the resources used in the post reform period and hence, the results of the study are in tune with the available literature. Thus, the majority of the manufacturing sector is facing the challenges of open internal and external competition in a bold manner.

TABLE 3.1-RESPONSE OF DAIRY PRODUCTS

	1999-02 – 1990-93			1995-98 – 1990-93			1999-02 – 1995-98		
Variables	**Mean Difference**	**t-value**	**Significance Level**	**Mean Difference**	**t-value**	**Significance Level**	**Mean Difference**	**t-value**	**Significance Level**
RMs/Net Sales	-0.10558	-2.941	*	-1.27E-02	-0.707		-9.28E-02	-3.531	*
W&S/Net Sales	1.76E-02	4.841	*	-2.89E-03	-1.395		2.05-02	12.337	* **
P&F/Net Sales	-6.49E-03	-9.925	* **	-7.31E-03	-41.779	* **	1.01E-03	1.235	
Adv/Net Sales	1.39E-02	2.264		-3.67E-03	-2.543		1.96E-02	3.544	*

@ Values could not be computed because the standard error of the difference is zero'
**Significant at 5 percent   **Significant al 1 percent*

TABLE 3.2-RESPONSE OF TEA AND COFFEE

	1999-02 – 1990-93			1995-98 – 1990-93			1999-02 – 1995-98		
Variables	**Mean Difference**	**t-value**	**Significance Level**	**Mean Difference**	**t-value**	**Significance Level**	**Mean Difference**	**t-value**	**Significance Level**
RMs/Net Sales	-7.39E-02	-9.275	* **	-1.87E-02	-0.276		-5.52E-02	-0.81	
W&S/Net Sales	0.106893	8.65	* **	2.81 E-02	1.191		7.88E-02	4.539	*
P&F/Net Sales	2.86E-02	11.853	* **	1.09E-02	2.475		1.77E-02	5.014	*
Adv/Net Sales	5.39E-03	5.872	*	3.90E-03	1.346		1.49E-03	0.714	

**Significant at 5 percent **Significant al 1 percent*

TABLE 3.3-RESPONSE OF SUGAR

	1999-02 – 1990-93			1995-98 – 1990-93			1999-02 – 1995-98		
Variables	**Mean Difference**	**t-value**	**Significance Level**	**Mean Difference**	**t-value**	**Significance Level**	**Mean Difference**	**t-value**	**Significance Level**
RMs/Net Sales	9.85E-03	0.51		-2.10E-02	-0.914		3.09E-02	1.045	
W&S/Net Sales	-2.01 E-02	-2.833		-1.47E-02	-9.723	* **	-5.41E-03	-0.629	
P&F/Net Sales	- 1.40E-02	-8.79	* **	-1.25E-02	- 17.959	* **	-1.47E-03	-0.81	
Adv/Net Sales	-2.35E-05	-0.916		7.89E-05	0.912		- 1.02E-04	-1.232	

**Significant at 5 percent* ***Significant al 1 percent*

TABLE 3.4-RESPONSE OF VEGETABLES OILS AND PRODUCTS

	1999-02 – 1990-93			1995-98 – 1990-93			1999-02 – 1995-98		
Variables	**Mean Difference**	**t-value**	**Significance Level**	**Mean Difference**	**t-value**	**Significance Level**	**Mean Difference**	**t-value**	**Significance Level**
RMs/Net Sales	2.76E-02	6.05	*	2.65E-02	5.047	*	1.11E-03	0.354	
W&S/Net Sales	-7.08 E -03	-14.789	* **	-1.03E-02	-7.36	* **	3.27E-03	2.478	
P&F/Net Sales	-7.33 E -03	-3.952	*	-6.48E-03	-2.677		-8.46E-04	-0.513	
Adv/Net Sales	5.16 E -03	4.912	*	1.74E-03	1.762		3.41E-03	2.203	

**Significant at 5 percent* ***Significant al 1 percent*

TABLE 3.5-RESPONSE OF BEVERAGES AND TOBACCO

	1999-02 – 1990-93			1995-98 – 1990-93			1999-02 – 1995-98		
Variables	**Mean Difference**	**t-value**	**Significance Level**	**Mean Difference**	**t-value**	**Significance Level**	**Mean Difference**	**t-value**	**Significance Level**
RMs/Net Sales	-0.13812	-10.199	* **	-6.71E-02	-5.193	*	-7.11E-02	-64.13	* **
W&S/Net Sales	1.72E-02	3.874	*	3.85E-03	1.295		1.33E-02	7.491	* **
P&F/Net Sales	8.44E-06	0.007		-3.03E-03	-2.948	*	3.04E-03	7.484	* **
Adv/Net Sales	2.26E-02	11.67	* **	2.47E-02	15.841	* *	-2.15E-03	-5.697	*

***Significant at 5 percent* ***Significant al 1 percent*

TABLE 3.6- RESPONSE OF COTTON TEXTILES

	1999-02 – 1990-93			1995-98 – 1990-93			1999-02 – 1995-98		
Variables	**Mean Difference**	**t-value**	**Significance Level**	**Mean Difference**	**t-value**	**Significance Level**	**Mean Difference**	**t-value**	**Significance Level**
RMs/Net Sales	2.92E-02	2.525		4.93E-02	1.736		-2.01E-02	-1.17	
W&S/Net Sales	-6.16E-02	-6.745	*	-5.90E-02	-4.095	*	-2.53E-03	-0.476	
P&F/Net Sales	7.15E-03	1.797		-6.81E-03	-1.099		1.40E-02	3.825	*
Adv/Net Sales	1.30E-03	3.173	*	7.52E-04	6.298	*	5.53E-04	1.062	

**Significant at 5 percent* ***Significant al 1 percent*

TABLE 3.7- RESPONSE OF SYNTHETIC TEXTILES

	1999-02 – 1990-93			1995-98 – 1990-93			1999-02 – 1995-98		
Variables	Mean Difference	t-value	Significance Level	Mean Difference	t-value	Significance Level	Mean Difference	t-value	Significance Level
RMs/Net Sales	0.317092	1.778		0.308991	1.625		8.10E-03	0.634	
W&S/Net Sales	0.204651	0.993		2.18E-03	0.509		0.202473	1.001	
P&F/Net Sales	5.16E-03	3.077	*	8.07E-04	0.157		4.35E-03	1.156	
Adv/Net Sales	-1.95E-03	-4.174	*	-1.67E-03	-4.646	*	-2.84E-04	-2.577	

*Significant at 5 percent **Significant al 1 percent

TABLE 3.8- RESPONSE OF INORGANIC CHEMICALS

	1999-02 – 1990-93			1995-98 – 1990-93			1999-02 – 1995-98		
Variables	Mean Difference	t-value	Significance Level	Mean Difference	t-value	Significance Level	Mean Difference	t-value	Significance Level
RMs/Net Sales	-5.67E-02	-33. 142	* **	-5.26E-03	-0.244		-5.15E-02	-2.331	
W&S/Net Sales	2.57E-02	11.621	* **	8.00E-03	0.756		1.77E-02	1.852	
P&F/Net Sales	6.34E-02	10.485	* **	2.80E-02	1.646		3.53E-02	3.164	
Adv/Net Sales	5.44E-03	0.8 16		1.28E-02	12.896	* **	-7.39E-03	-1.224	

**Significant at 5 percent* ***Significant al 1 percent*

TABLE 3.9-RESPONSE OF ALKALIES

	1999-02 – 1990-93			1995-98 – 1990-93			1999-02 – 1995-98		
Variables	**Mean Difference**	**t-value**	**Significance Level**	**Mean Difference**	**t-value**	**Significance Level**	**Mean Difference**	**t-value**	**Significance Level**
RMs/Net Sales	0.142841	8.574	* **	2.68E-02	1.401		0.1 16077	4.999	
W&S/Net Sales	3.00E-02	12.604	* **	2.68E-02	3.633	*	3.18E-03	0.351	
P&F/Net Sales	8.17E-02	5.686	*	5.79E-02	2.126		2.38E-02	0.959	
Adv/Net Sales	-6.63E-04	-1.392		-4.63E-04	- 1.176		-2.00E-04	-1.409	

**Significant at 5 percent* ***Significant al 1 percent*

TABLE 3.10- RESPONSE OF FERTILIZERS

	1999-02 – 1990-93			1995-98 – 1990-93			1999-02 – 1995-98		
Variables	**Mean Difference**	**t-value**	**Significance Level**	**Mean Difference**	**t-value**	**Significance Level**	**Mean Difference**	**t-value**	**Significance Level**
RMs/Net Sales	3.10E-02	0.816		2.88E-03	0.059		2.8 1E-02	1.78	
W&S/Net Sales	9.97E-03	7.463	* **	8.99E-03	4.564	*	9.82E-04	1.398	
P&F/Net Sales	2.39E-02	2.292		9.14E-03	1.328		I .47E-02	2.03 1	
Adv/Net Sales	-2.82E-04	-0.944		4.25E-04	2.558		-7.07E-04	-1.538	

**Significant at 5 percent* ***Significant al 1 percent*

TABLE 3.11-RESPONSE OF PESTICIDES

	1999-02 – 1990-93			1995-98 – 1990-93			1999-02 – 1995-98		
Variables	Mean Difference	t-value	Significance Level	Mean Difference	t-value	Significance Level	Mean Difference	t-value	Significance
RMs/Net Sales	-1.10E-02	-1.362		2.23E-02	1.955		-3.33E-02	-1.788	
W&S/Net Sales	-2.09E-02	-8.678	* **	-1.86E-02	-3.625	*	-2.33E-03	-0.462	
P&F/Net Sales	1.70E-03	4.095	*	-3.23E-03	-6.005	*	4.93E-03	39.286	* **
Adv/Net Sales	6.49E-03	7.977	* **	5.98E-03	4.86	*	5.12E-04	0.258	

**Significant at 5 percent* ***Significant al 1 percent*

TABLE 3.12- RESPONSE OF PAINTS AND VARNISHES

	1999-02 – 1990-93			1995-98 – 1990-93			1999-02 – 1995-98		
Variables	Mean Difference	t-value	Significance Level	Mean Difference	t-value	Significance Level	Mean Difference	t-value	Significance Level
RMs/Net Sales	-5.61E-02	-10.775	* **	-1.14E-02	-0.914		-4.48E-02	-2.979	*
W&S/Net Sales	3.93E-03	1.414		-6.15E-05	-0.029		3.99E-03	2.338	
P&F/Net Sales	-4.0 1E-03	-18.978	* **	6.60E-04	0.723		-4.67E-03	-4.201	*
Adv/Net Sales	-1.31E-02	-4.842	*	-6.86E-03	-3.291	*	-6.27E-03	-6.22	*

**Significant at 5 percent* ***Significant al 1 percent*

TABLE 3.13- RESPONSE OF DYES AND PIGMENTS

	1999-02 – 1990-93			1995-98 – 1990-93			1999-02 – 1995-98		
Variables	**Mean Difference**	**t-value**	**Significance Level**	**Mean Difference**	**t-value**	**Significance Level**	**Mean Difference**	**t-value**	**Significance Level**
RMs/Net Sales	-2.76E-02	-0.781		-5.72E-03	-0.135		-2.19E-02	-3.117	*
W&S/Net Sales	1.44E-02	2.65		2.29E-03	0.334		1.21E-02	7.812	* **
P&F/Net Sales	-7.23E-03	-2.19		-1.67E-02	-2.137		9.51E-03	2.081	
Adv/Net Sales	5.83E-04	5.424	*	6.24E-04	4.388	*	-4.06E-05	-0.217	

**Significant at 5 percent   **Significant al 1 percent*

TABLE 3.14- RESPONSE OF DRUGS AND PHARMACEUTICALS

	1999-02 – 1990-93			1995-98 – 1990-93			1999-02 – 1995-98		
Variables	**Mean Difference**	**t-value**	**Significance Level**	**Mean Difference**	**t-value**	**Significance Level**	**Mean Difference**	**t-value**	**Significance Level**
RMs/Net Sales	-4.57E-02	-2.218		-0.19855	-1.219		0.152807	0.844	
W&S/Net Sales	-2.38E-02	-4.613	*	-2.05E-02	-2.965	*	-3.31E-03	-1.462	
P&F/Net Sales	-4.19E-03	-2.618		-2.38E-03	-4.672	*	-1.81E-03	-0.882	
Adv/Net Sales	-9.84E-04	-1.656		-6.00E-04	-0.798		-3.84E-04	-0.318	

**Significant at 5 percent,* ***Significant al 1 percent*

TABLE 3.15- RESPONSE OF SOAPS AND DETERGENTS

	1999-02 – 1990-93			1995-98 – 1990-93			1999-02 – 1995-98		
Variables	**Mean Difference**	**t-value**	**Significance Level**	**Mean Difference**	**t-value**	**Significance Level**	**Mean Difference**	**t-value**	**Significance Level**
RMs/Net Sales	-4.1 7E-03	-0.194		1 .32E-02	2.031		-1.74E-02	-0.797	
W&S/Net Sales	3.45E-04	0.058		-3.56E-04	-0.075		7.0lE-04	0.57	
P&F/Net Sales	2.63E-02	4.971	*	2.65E-03	0.63		2.37E-02	19.014	* **
Adv/Net Sales	1.18E-02	1.936		-2.03E-03	-1.244		1.38E-02	2.322	

**Significant at 5 percent* ***Significant al 1 percent*

TABLE 3.16- RESPONSE OF COSMETICS AND TOILETRIES

	1999-02 – 1990-93			1995-98 – 1990-93			1999-02 – 1995-98		
Variables	**Mean Difference**	**t-value**	**Significance Level**	**Mean Difference**	**t-value**	**Significance Level**	**Mean Difference**	**t-value**	**Significance Level**
RMs/Net Sales	-0.10713	-10.553	* **	-0.43753	-55.445	* **	0.330398	58.131	* **
W&S/Net Sales	0.106247	1.048		0.537149	52.843	* **	-0.430903	-4.585	*
P&F/Net Sales	4.26E-03	12.404	* **	4.28E-02	26.165	* **	-3.86E-02	-19.922	* **
Adv/Net Sales	6.41E-02	17.539	* **	5.92E-02	9.875	* **	4.91E-03	0.509	

**Significant at 5 percent* ***Significant al 1 percent*

TABLE 3.17- RESPONSE OF ORGANIC CHEMICALS

	1999-02 – 1990-93			1995-98 – 1990-93			1999-02 – 1995-98		
Variables	**Mean Difference**	**t-value**	**Significance Level**	**Mean Difference**	**t-value**	**Significance Level**	**Mean Difference**	**t-value**	**Significance Level**
RMs/Net Sales	6.41E-02	2.752		4.18E-02	51.815	* **	2.23E-02	0.963	
W&S/Net Sales	1.67E-03	1.379		-2.00E-03	-0.57		3.67E-03	1.574	
P&F/Net Sales	5.98E-03	0.972		-6.82E-03	-0.984		1.28E-02	3.032	*
Adv/Net Sales	-2.32E-04	-2.935	*	8.82E-05	1.058		-3.20E-04	-2.777	

**Significant at 5 percent* ***Significant al 1 percent*

TABLE 3.18- RESPONSE OF POLYMERS

	1999-02 – 1990-93			1995-98 – 1990-93			1999-02 – 1995-98		
Variables	**Mean Difference**	**t-value**	**Significance Level**	**Mean Difference**	**t-value**	**Significance Level**	**Mean Difference**	**t-value**	**Significance Level**
RMs/Net Sales	7.04E-02	4.439	*	-5.24E-03	-0.255		7.56E-02	2.374	
W&S/Net Sales	7.51E-03	1.722		1.13E-02	12.026	* **	-3.78E-03	-0.762	
P&F/Net Sales	8.32E-03	1.02		-4.43E-03	-0.463		1.28E-02	1.139	
Adv/Net Sales	-4.30E-04	-0.845		-1.14E-04	-0.179		-3.15E-04	-0.646	

**Significant at 5 percent* ***Significant al 1 percent*

TABLE 3.19- RESPONSE OF PLASTIC PRODUCTS

	1999-02 – 1990-93			1995-98 – 1990-93			1999-02 – 1995-98		
Variables	**Mean Difference**	**t-value**	**Significance Level**	**Mean Difference**	**t-value**	**Significance Level**	**Mean Difference**	**t-value**	**Significance Level**
RMs/Net Sales	-2.57E-02	-8.004	* **	1.71E-02	1.593		-3.52E-02	-78.901	* **
W&S/Net Sales	-7.86E-04	-0.301		-9.69E-03	-2.287		7.29E-03	5.182	*
P&F/Net Sales	2.51E-02	31.096	* **	7.40E-03	1.451		1.30E-02	3.166	*
Adv/Net Sales	1.42E-05	0.05		-1.36E-03	-0.766		2.29E-03	0.985	

**Significant at 5 percent* ***Significant al 1 percent*

TABLE 3.20- RESPONSE OF PETROLEUM PRODUCTS

	1999-02 – 1990-93			1995-98 – 1990-93			1999-02 – 1995-98		
Variables	**Mean Difference**	**t-value**	**Significance Level**	**Mean Difference**	**t-value**	**Significance Level**	**Mean Difference**	**t-value**	**Significance Level**
RMs/Net Sales	0.130906	23.117	* **	3.27E-02	1.937		9.82E-02	6.327	*
W&S/Net Sales	1.56E-03	2.197		2.07E-03	1.388		-5.06E-04	-0.362	
P&F/Net Sales	7.41E-03	5.85	*	-3.21E-03	-3.228	*	1.06E-02	14.475	* **
Adv/Net Sales	2.93E-04	13.421	* **	5.12E-04	2.565		-2.19E-04	-1.233	

**Significant at 5 percent* ***Significant al 1 percent*

TABLE 3.21- RESPONSE OF TYRES AND TUBES

	1999-02 – 1990-93			1995-98 – 1990-93			1999-02 – 1995-98		
Variables	Mean Difference	t-value	Significance Level	Mean Difference	t-value	Significance Level	Mean Difference	t-value	Significance Level
RMs/Net Sales	-3.47E-02	-3.496	*	3.46E-03	0.145		-3.82E-02	-2.327	
W&S/Net Sales	8.45E-03	2.985	*	-6.10E-03	-2.467		1.45E-02	4.305	*
P&F/Net Sales	1.46E-02	3.345	*	8.79E-04	0.772		1.37E-02	3.511	*
Adv/Net Sales	1.11E-03	0.647		-1.55E-03	-1.684		2.66E-03	1.139	

**Significant at 5 percent* ***Significant al 1 percent*

Table-3.22 – RESPONSE OF RUBBER AND RUBBER PRODUCTS

	1999-02-1990-93			1995-98-1990-93			1999-02-1995-98		
Variables	**Mean Difference**	**t-value**	**Significance Level**	**Mean Difference**	**t-value**	**Significance Level**	**Mean Difference**	**t-value**	**Significance Level**
RMs/Net Sales	-7.00E-02	-16.667	* **	-3.61E-02	-2.269		-3.39E-02	-2.368	
W&S/Net Sales	6.03E-03	1.693		-1.55E-02	-1.407		2.15E-02	2.502	
P&F/Net Sales	5.56E-03	0.738		-1.25E-02	-1.14		1.80E-02	3.353	*
Adv/Net Sales	4.85E-03	6.71	*	1.72E-03	1.091		3.13E-03	2.33	

**Significant at 5 percent* ***Significant al 1 percent*

TABLE- 3.23- RESPONSE OF CEMENT

	1999-02-1990-93			1995-98-1990-93			1999-02-1995-98		
Variables	**Mean Difference**	**t-value**	**Significance Level**	**Mean Difference**	**t-value**	**Significance Level**	**Mean Difference**	**t-value**	**Significance Level**
RMs/Net Sales	-1.06E-02	-1.532		-1.48E-02	-2.17		4.23E-03	0.71	
W&S/Net Sales	1.37E-04	0.041		2.85E-03	0.547		-2.71E-03	-0.429	
P&F/Net Sales	3.72E-02	1.63		3.70E-02	5.516	*	2.00E-04	0.007	
Adv/Net Sales	6.28E-02	1.079		3.41E-03	25.808	* **	5.94E-02	1.023	

**Significant at 5 percent* ***Significant al 1 percent*

TABLE 3.24 RESPONSE OF PIG IRON AND SPONGE IRON

	1999-02-1990-93			1995-98-1990-93			1999-02-1995-98		
Variables	**Mean Difference**	**t-value**	**Significance Level**	**Mean Difference**	**t-value**	**Significance Level**	**Mean Difference**	**t-value**	**Significance Level**
RMs/Net Sales	8.39E-02	2.395		0.100251	4.53	*	-1.64E-02	-1.269	
W&S/Net Sales	2.37E-02	34.425	* **	6.93E-03	2.704		0.580261	68.037	* **
P&F/Net Sales	5.08E-04	0.182		1.60E-02	2.59		-1.54E-02	-3.938	*
Adv/Net Sales	-3.73E-03	-1.014		-3.40E-03	-0.893		-3.35E-04	-2.118	

**Significant at 5 percent* ***Significant al 1 percent*

TABLE 3.25- RESPONSE OF STEEL

	1999-02-1990-93			1995-98-1990-93			1999-02-1995-98		
Variables	**Mean Difference**	**t-value**	**Significance Level**	**Mean Difference**	**t-value**	**Significance Level**	**Mean Difference**	**t-value**	**Significance Level**
RMs/Net Sales	3.05E-02	5.506	*	4.58E-02	5.345	*	-1.52E-02	-2.644	
W&S/Net Sales	4.84E-032	1.136		-3.65E-03	-1.115		8.48E-03	7.972	* **
P&F/Net Sales	2.67E-02	31.045	* **	1.57E-02	2.584		1.10E-02	1.911	
Adv/Net Sales	-6.27E-05	-3.527	*	8.24E-05	1.333		-1.45E-04	-1.944	

**Significant at 5 percent **Significant al 1 percent*

TABLE 3.26 RESPONSE OF FERRO ALLOYS

	1999-02-1990-93			1995-98-1990-93			1999-02-1995-98		
Variables	**Mean Difference**	**t-value**	**Significance Level**	**Mean Difference**	**t-value**	**Significance Level**	**Mean Difference**	**t-value**	**Significance Level**
RMs/Net Sales	8.09E-03	0.752		2.21E-03	0.102		5.88E-03	0.527	
W&S/Net Sales	6.69E-03	2.083		-5.56E-03	-0.424		1.23E-02	1.134	
P&F/Net Sales	-9.23E-03	-0.507		-1.20E-02	-0.397		2.74E-03	0.146	
Adv/Net Sales	-9.81E-05	-2.263		-2.21E-05	-0.33		-7.60E-5	-2.64	

**Significant at 5 percent* ***Significant al 1 percent*

TABLE-3.27- RESPONSE OF CASTINGS AND FORGINGS

	1999-02-1990-93			1995-98-1990-93			1999-02-1995-98		
Variables	**Mean Difference**	**t-value**	**Significance Level**	**Mean Difference**	**t-value**	**Significance Level**	**Mean Difference**	**t-value**	**Significance Level**
RMs/Net Sales	1.32E-02	5.213	*	7.00E-02	4.979	*	-5.68E-02	-4.385	*
W&S/Net Sales	-3.11E-02	-23.429	* **	-2.15E-02	-3.759	*	-9.69E-03	-1.384	
P&F/Net Sales	1.34E-02	2.157		-2.74E-03	-3.18	*	1.61E-02	2.282	
Adv/Net Sales	9.67E-05	4.944	*	5.96E-04	1.806		-4.99E-04	-1.594	

**Significant at 5 percent*   ***Significant al 1 percent*

TABLE 3.28- RESPONSE OF METAL PRODUCTS

	1999-02-1990-93			1995-98-1990-93			1999-02-1995-98		
Variables	**Mean Difference**	**t-value**	**Significance Level**	**Mean Difference**	**t-value**	**Significance Level**	**Mean Difference**	**t-value**	**Significance Level**
RMs/Net Sales	-4.72E-02	-5.565	*	-4.30E-02	-4.147	*	-4.21E-03	-0.36	
W&S/Net Sales	-9.44E-03	-8.985	* **	9.69E-03	2.604		-1.91E-02	-4.149	*
P&F/Net Sales	7.15E-03	2.935	*	1.75E-03	0.488		5.40E-03	4.484	*
Adv/Net Sales	2.67E-03	3.007	*	2.36E-03	2.153		3.08E-04	0.954	

**Significant at 5 percent* ***Significant al 1 percent*

TABLE-3.29- RESPONSE OF NON FERROUS METALS

	1999-02-1990-93			1995-98-1990-93			1999-02-1995-98		
Variables	**Mean Difference**	**t-value**	**Significance Level**	**Mean Difference**	**t-value**	**Significance Level**	**Mean Difference**	**t-value**	**Significance Level**
RMs/Net Sales	9.35E-02	10.891	* **	6.22E-02	2.965	*	3.13E-02	1.311	
W&S/Net Sales	-6.41E-03	-3.118	*	-8.48E-03	-1.587		2.08E-03	0.281	
P&F/Net Sales	-4.19E-02	-34.374	* **	-3.29E-02	-2.51		-8.95E-03	-0.748	
Adv/Net Sales	-2.95E-04	-1.058		-4.29E-05	-0.155		-2.52E-04	-7.943	* **

**Significant at 5 percent* ***Significant al 1 percent*

TABLE 3.30 RESPONSE OF NON ELECTRICAL MACHINERY

	1999-02-1990-93			1995-98-1990-93			1999-02-1995-98		
Variables	**Mean Difference**	**t-value**	**Significance Level**	**Mean Difference**	**t-value**	**Significance Level**	**Mean Difference**	**t-value**	**Significance Level**
RMs/Net Sales	-4.12E-02	-4.357	*	-3.38E-02	-7.172	* **	-7.48E-03	-0.531	
W&S/Net Sales	3.42E-02	2.376		1.78E-03	0.419		3.24E-02	1.834	
P&F/Net Sales	6.24E-03	7.387	* **	3.11E-03	6.672	*	3.13E-03	3.118	*
Adv/Net Sales	-1.10E-04	-0.191		-1.36E-04	-0.405		2.53E-05	0.103	

**Significant at 5 percent*　　***Significant al 1 percent*

TABLE 3.31- RESPONSE OF ELECTRICAL MACHINERY

	1999-02-1990-93			1995-98-1990-93			1999-02-1995-98		
Variables	**Mean Difference**	**t-value**	**Significance Level**	**Mean Difference**	**t-value**	**Significance Level**	**Mean Difference**	**t-value**	**Significance Level**
RMs/Net Sales	1.13E-02	0.87		2.41E-02	2.632		6.63E-03	0.441	
W&S/Net Sales	-3.18E-02	-68.739	* **	-3.01E-02	-4.361	*	-8.55E-03	-2.613	
P&F/Net Sales	2.94E-03	1.974		-1.03E-03	-0.661		2.21E-03	0.574	
Adv/Net Sales	7.80E-03	12.946	* **	8.28E-03	10.487	* **	-5.08E-05	-0.024	

**Significant at 5 percent* ***Significant al 1 percent*

TABLE 3.32- RESPONSE OF ELECTRONICS

	1999-02-1990-93			1995-98-1990-93			1999-02-1995-98		
Variables	Mean Difference	t-value	Significance Level	Mean Difference	t-value	Significance Level	Mean Difference	t-value	Significance Level
RMs/Net Sales	-0.1841	-7.422	* **	-1.69E-02	-0.621		-0.167185	-44.277	* **
W&S/Net Sales	4.13E-02	2.796		-7.34E-03	-1.645		4.86E-02	4.718	*
P&F/Net Sales	-1.42E-03	-4.471	*	-2.63E-04	-1.359		-1.16E-03	-5.074	*
Adv/Net Sales	1.12E-03	0.76		7.83E-03	4.575	*	-6.71E-03	-4.553	*

*Significant at 5 percent **Significant al 1 percent

TABLE 3.33 – RESPONSE OF TRANSPORT EQUIPMENT

	1999-02-1990-93			1995-98-1990-93			1999-02-1995-98		
Variables	**Mean Difference**	**t-value**	**Significance Level**	**Mean Difference**	**t-value**	**Significance Level**	**Mean Difference**	**t-value**	**Significance Level**
RMs/Net Sales	-1.08E-02	-0.773		-4.99E-03	-0.228		-5.77E-03	-0.343	
W&S/Net Sales	-3.24E-02	-6.481	*	-2.76E-02	-19.698	* **	-4.78E-033	-0.824	
P&F/Net Sales	2.32E-03	1.552		2.05E-03	4.972	*	2.61E-04	0.223	
Adv/Net Sales	7.25E-03	8.03	* **	1.87E-03	2.832		5.38E-03	7.541	* **

**Significant at 5 percent* ***Significant al 1 percent*

TABLE 3.34- RESPONSE OF AUTOMOBILES

	1999-02-1990-93			1995-98-1990-93			1999-02-1995-98		
Variables	**Mean Difference**	**t-value**	**Significance Level**	**Mean Difference**	**t-value**	**Significance Level**	**Mean Difference**	**t-value**	**Significance Level**
RMs/Net Sales	0.194518	1.008		0.201978	0.945		-7.46E-03	-0.346	
W&S/Net Sales	-1.75E-03	-0.044		7.94E-03	0.206		-9.69E-03	-1.462	
P&F/Net Sales	2.81E-03	0.439		4.23E-03	0.729		-1..41E-03	-1.322	
Adv/Net Sales	1.15E-02	39.483	* **	4.01E-03	4.752	*	7.48E-03	7.542	* **

**Significant at 5 percent N* ***Significant al 1 percent*

TABLE 3.35- RESPONSE OF AUTOMOBILE ANCILLIARIES

	1999-02-1990-93			1995-98-1990-93			1999-02-1995-98		
Variables	**Mean Difference**	**t-value**	**Significance Level**	**Mean Difference**	**t-value**	**Significance Level**	**Mean Difference**	**t-value**	**Significance Level**
RMs/Net Sales	4.21E-04	0.081		-8.03E-03	-2.076		8.45E-03	1.433	
W&S/Net Sales	-1.14E-02	-4.935	*	-2.01E-02	-2.424		8.74E-03	1.455	
P&F/Net Sales	1.48E-02	10.541	* **	1.11E-02	11.142	* **	3.67E-03	1.565	
Adv/Net Sales	-4.31E-04	-1.02		-1.64E-04	-0.325		-2.68E-04	-1.766	

**Significant at 5 percent* ***Significant al 1 percent*

TABLE 3.36- RESONSE OF PAPER AND PAPER PRODUCTS

	1999-02-1990-93			1995-98-1990-93			1999-02-1995-98		
Variables	**Mean Difference**	**t-value**	**Significance Level**	**Mean Difference**	**t-value**	**Significance Level**	**Mean Difference**	**t-value**	**Significance Level**
RMs/Net Sales	2.21E-02	3.932	*	1.86E-02	4.096	*	3.46E-03	3.235	*
W&S/Net Sales	-9.46E-04	-0.547		-7.80E-03	-2.152		6.85E-03	1.37	
P&F/Net Sales	-8.36E-03	-0.743		5.43E-03	0.439		-1.38E-02	-0.586	
Adv/Net Sales	3.34E-05	0.677		6.74E-04	1.83		-6.41E-04	-1.947	

**Significant at 5 percent* ***Significant al 1 percent*

TABLE 3.37 – RESPONSE OF LEATHER PRODUCTS

	1999-02-1990-93			1995-98-1990-93			1999-02-1995-98		
Variables	**Mean Difference**	**t-value**	**Significance Level**	**Mean Difference**	**t-value**	**Significance Level**	**Mean Difference**	**t-value**	**Significance Level**
RMs/Net Sales	3.26E-02	1.282		-0.11661	-0.59		0.149249	0.68	
W&S/Net Sales	-5.30E-02	-2.854		-0.10843	-2.735		5.54E-02	1.843	
P&F/Net Sales	4.15E-03	1.373		-8.70E-03	-1.483		1.28E-02	2.808	
Adv/Net Sales	-1.90E-03	-0.757		-6.04E-03	-1.815		4.14E-03	1.623	

**Significant at 5 percent* ***Significant al 1 percent*

TABLE 3.38 RESPONSE OF BOOKS AND NEWSPAPERS

	1999-02-1990-93			1995-98-1990-93			1999-02-1995-98		
Variables	Mean Difference	t-value	Significance Level	Mean Difference	t-value	Significance Level	Mean Difference	t-value	Significance Level
RMs/Net Sales	-3.72E-02	-1.162		-1.41E-02	-1.884		-2.31E-02	-0.894	
W&S/Net Sales	-1.67E-02	-25.816	* **	-1.87E-02	-2.485		2.01E-03	0.248	
P&F/Net Sales	2.75E-03	5.426	*	4.71E-04	0.556		2.28E-03	4.365	*
Adv/Net Sales	8.77E-03	11.881	* **	1.36E-02	1.967		-4.83E-03	-0.705	

**Significant at 5 percent* ***Significant al 1 percent*

TABLE 3.39 RESPONSE OF WOOD

	1999-02-1990-93			1995-98-1990-93			1999-02-1995-98		
Variables	**Mean Difference**	**t-value**	**Significance Level**	**Mean Difference**	**t-value**	**Significance Level**	**Mean Difference**	**t-value**	**Significance Level**
RMs/Net Sales	-1.53E-02	-1.498		-4.40E-02	-2.308		2.88E-02	1.011	
W&S/Net Sales	9.17E-03	3.484	*	-7.28E-03	-2.924	*	1.64E-02	3.982	*
P&F/Net Sales	2.20E-02	10.15	* **	8.68E-04	0.254		2.11E-02	5.429	*
Adv/Net Sales	5.30E-03	6.788	*	6.13E-03	3.928	*	-8.23E-04	-0.455	

**Significant at 5 percent* ***Significant al 1 percent*

TABLE 3.40 – RESPONSE OF CLOCKS AND WATCHES

	1999-02-1990-93			1995-98-1990-93			1999-02-1995-98		
Variables	**Mean Difference**	**t-value**	**Significance Level**	**Mean Difference**	**t-value**	**Significance Level**	**Mean Difference**	**t-value**	**Significance Level**
RMs/Net Sales	-5.81E-02	-1.427		-6.83-02	-1.424		1.02E-02	0.271	
W&S/Net Sales	8.66E-02	4.368	*	3.77E-02	3.839	*	4.89E-02	2.06	
P&F/Net Sales	-1.98956	-6.104	*	-3.00685	-12.371	* **	1.017288	8.869	* **
Adv/Net Sales	-9.31E-03	-1.423		-2.16E-03	-0.145		-7.15E-03	-0.863	

**Significant at 5 percent* ***Significant al 1 percent*

TABLE 3.41 RESPONSE OF DIVERSIFIED

	1999-02-1990-93			1995-98-1990-93			1999-02-1995-98		
Variables	**Mean Difference**	**t-value**	**Significance Level**	**Mean Difference**	**t-value**	**Significance Level**	**Mean Difference**	**t-value**	**Significance Level**
RMs/Net Sales	7.93E-02	1.961		1.83E-02	1.421		6.10E-02	2.201	
W&S/Net Sales	-5.51E-02	-16.18	* **	-3.55E-02	-11.623	* **	-1.96E-02	-3.047	*
P&F/Net Sales	-8.67E-03	-0.724		6.33E-03	1.003		-1.50E-02	-2.425	
Adv/Net Sales	7.53E-03	5.566	*	5.13E-03	1.788		2.40E-03	0.576	

**Significant at 5 percent* ***Significant al 1 percent*

Chapter IV

SUMMARY AND CONCLUSIONS

Section I Summary

Efficient use of resources is known to make imperative differences in the productivity of the nations. Two nations with same resources and the same skills can have different production levels due to the differences in the efficiency of the resources. A nation, which is using its resources efficiently, making minimal wastage and using the better quality inputs etc., can make differences in the output levels and therefore it can march ahead of other nations. Developing nations that are in short of resources, have varying demands and have huge numbers to feed are directly affected by the efficient use of the resources. As discussed in Chapter I, efficient use of the resources received attention very late and since then almost all the economists have come to believe that the efficient use of the resources can make huge differences in the standard of living of the people by providing them with the increased number of goods at their disposal and thereby increasing their surplus.

Efficiency may reflect in- reductions in the costs and the improvement in the quality of the goods. Though it can happen that in the beginning only reductions in the costs are experienced but in the long run, with open competition, improvements in the quality of the goods would have to be there because the forces of competition would throw out the firm that is supplying poor quality goods. Efficiency, therefore, implies the movement of the economy from any point under the production possibility curve to any point on the production function. Efficiency can also be described in terms of the inputs used in the process of production. The problems associated with defining and measuring the efficiency of capital are discussed in detail in chapter I because of which the same variable could not be measured in the present study. Thus, the present study covered the measurement of the efficiency in the use of labour, raw materials, power and fuel, and advertising costs. Following variables were estimated- raw materials cost per rupee of sales (RMs/Net sales), wages and salaries cost per rupee of sales (W & S/Net sales), power and fuel cost per rupee of sales (P&F/Net sales), advertising cost per rupee of sales (Adv/Net sales). Difference of means test was employed to see whether there have been any significant changes in various components of average variable cost of production. And then a comparison of the average values of various variables for 1999-2000, 2000-2001, 2001 - 2002 (latter part of the decade of reform period) with average values of various variables for 1990-91,1991-92,1992-93 (pre reform period), and average values of various variables for 1995-96, 1996-97, 1997-98 (mid of decade of reform period) with average values of various variables for 1990-91,1991-92,1992-93 (pre reform period) and average values of various variables for 1999-2000, 2000-2001, 2001- 2002 (latter part of the decade of reform period) with average values of various variables for 1995-96, 1996-97, 1997-98 (mid of decade of reform period). Data source have been accessed from CMIE and 41 industries were chosen.

Before the empirical analysis, a theoretical discussion of the pre reform industrial policy and the policy being followed after 1990-91 revealed that before the introduction of the reforms there were a number of policies, acts that restricted both the foreign and the internal competition. Some such policies were Industries Act of 1951, Essential Commodities Act, Monopolies and Restrictive Trade Practices Act, etc. In addition to these there were barriers to exit and barriers for the entry of the firms both foreign and Indian and on the Indian firms going global. These restrictions were in the form of Import Control Act, controls on exports and foreign technology and on foreign collaborations. As a result of these controls the Indian government created an industrial sector with rampant oligopolies, where existence of the sub-optimal capacities was a rule rather than exception, forced the producers to substitute poor quality or the expensive raw material, poor capacity utilisation, use of out-dated technology, which ultimately lead to a great loss in the consumer and the producer surplus. As a result of huge inefficiency in the industrial sector, its own growth was affected negatively and in turn whole of the economy was affected adversely. This along with various other factors, pushed India to the brink of the economic crisis and as a result of this, reforms were introduced which reduced the level of government intervention in the industry by abolishing the various regulatory and control acts and opening up the economy. As a result the economy was expected to steer clear of the wide spread inefficiencies and was expected to face the challenges of the open competition boldly.

Section II Conclusions

The analysis of the 41 industries revealed that:

- Out of the 41 industries, 27 industries responded as per the hypothesis. These were:

1. Dairy Products,
2. Tea and Coffee,
3. Sugar,
4. Vegetable oils and Products,
5. Beverages and Tobacco,
6. Cotton Textiles,
7. Inorganic Chemicals,
8. Pesticides,
9. Dyes and Pigments,
10. Paints and Varnishes,
11. Rubber and Rubber Products,
12. Drugs and Pharmaceuticals,
13. Cosmetics and Toiletries,
14. Plastic Products,
15. Petroleum,
16. Castings and Forgings,
17. Metal Products,
18. Non Ferrous Metals,
19. Electrical Machinery,
20. Non Electrical Machinery,
21. Electronics,
22. Transport Equipment,
23. Automobile,
24. Automobile Ancilliaries,
25. Books and Newspapers,
26. Clocks and Watches, and
27. Diversified.

- The response of 12 industries was not as per the hypothesis. These industries were:

1. Synthetic Textiles,
2. Alkalies,

3. Fertilizers,
4. Organic Chemicals,
5. Polymers,
6. Tyres and Tubes,
7. Soaps and Detergents,
8. Paper and Paper Products,
9. Cement,
10. Pig Iron and Sponge Iron,
11. Steel, and
12. Wood.

- Nine industries significantly reduced the share of power and fuel costs/net sales, and 18 industries were found to be experiencing the rising trend in these costs. This rise in power and fuel costs might be more for reasons of internationally increasing prices of fuel, charging of user prices by electricity boards after the introduction of the reforms, than reflecting inefficient use of this resource.
- Twelve industries reduced their rising share of raw material costs/net sales significantly. But 9 industries were unable to reduce the raw material costs
- Thirteen industries experienced significant reductions in wages and salaries costs/net sales. And 14 industries experienced rise in this variable, which, may tentatively be taken to indicate rising labour productivity.
- Advertising/net sales has increased significantly in most of the industries. As many as 19 industries spent more of their sales on advertising expenditure. This is, however, indicative of the rising resolve on the part of Indian business to create brand equity and enhance survivability to face the challenges of competing with MNCs.

The initial response of the Indian industries to the challenges thrown by the open and competitive regime shows that the Indian industrial sector is facing these challenges boldly and is better placed than earlier times but in the light of the increasing realisation of the imperativeness of India introducing further reforms, industrial sector needs to continually revise its mode of operations and their policies in order to match the standards of the foreign firms. Changes at the global level are bound to affect the Indian firms, efficient ones will utilise such opportunities to their advantage and the inefficient ones will give others an opportunity to others to take them over. With world becoming a smaller place, it is expected that the foreign firms will get increasing access to the Indian markets sooner or later. Indian industrial sector has very less time to restructure its operations in areas of production, marketing, advertising, distribution, etc, and prepare itself well to face the global competitors.

APPENDIX 1

TABLE 1. 1- FINANCIAL RAITOS FOR DAIRY PRODUCT

Variables	1990-91	1991-92	1992-93	1995-96	1996-97	1997-98	1999-00	2000-01	2001-02
RMs/Net Sales	0.6920259	0.7317708	0.702529168	0.709622	0.6870078	0.691466	0.6567283	0.6038168	0.5490492
W&S/Net Sales	0.043473	0.0463362	0.04494558	0.037377	0.0427987	0.045923	0.0564526	0.0614439	0.697594
P&F/Net Sales	0.0376114	0.0356501	0.035079477	0.030441	0.0279932	0.027978	0.0298152	0.0335382	0.0341997
Adv/Net Sales	0.0344364	0.030352	0.032495498	0.028199	0.0268026	0.031259	0.0368717	0.0502302	0.0578402

TABLE 1.2- FINANCIAL RATIOS FOR TEA AND COFFEE

Variables	1990-91	1991-92	1992-93	1995-96	1996-97	1997-98	1999-00	2000-01	2001-02
RMs/Net Sales	0.351066	0.33182504	0.338583	0.4637471	0.275725	0.225884	0.273225	0.269336	0.25321
W&S/Net Sales	0.19978	0.20504441	0.221896	0.1870287	0.274103	0.2499	0.282846	0.31817	0.346384
P&F/Net Sales	0.03315	0.03699514	0.043783	0.0399801	0.056677	0.04994	0.057008	0.068672	0.074128
Adv/Net Sales	0.013102	0.01529244	0.017884	0.0227746	0.015773	0.019443	0.020105	0.019117	0.023226

TABLE 1.3- FINANCIAL RATIOS FOR SUGAR

Variables	1990-91	1991-92	1992-93	1995-96	1996-97	1997-98	1999-00	2000-01	2001-02
RMs/Net Sales	0.7646377	0.75704379	0.7104774	0.7729038	0.752106	0.644132	0.8050846	0.7311763	0.7254542
W&S/Net Sales	0.0943768	0.099655691	0.0953089	0.0766678	0.086247	0.082337	0.0884625	0.0722405	0.0683136
P&F/Net Sales	0.0292174	0.031957713	0.0310395	0.0162707	0.018508	0.019886	0.0183555	0.0158807	0.0160259
Adv/Net Sales	0.0002899	0.000242471	0.0003306	0.0002169	0.000469	0.000414	0.0002774	0.0002568	0.0002583

TABLE 1.4- FINANCIAL RATIOS FOR VEGETABLE OILS AND PRODUCTS

Variables	1990-91	1991-92	1992-93	1995-96	1996-97	1997-98	1999-00	2000-01	2001-02
RMs/Net Sales	0.854197	0.8460584	0.859874	0.8911629	0.867315	0.881074	0.889096	0.8747	0.879085
W&S/Net Sales	0.023834	0.02684936	0.023659	0.0146966	0.013698	0.014903	0.017711	0.019377	0.016028
P&F/Net Sales	0.029213	0.03535034	0.031364	0.0254286	0.024039	0.027017	0.025495	0.025485	0.022965
Adv/Net Sales	0.003586	0.00406568	0.004297	0.0035709	0.005904	0.007706	0.00808	0.011281	0.008061

TABLE 1.5- FINANCIAL RATIOS FOR BEVERAGES AND TOBACCO

Variables	1990-91	1991-92	1992-93	1995-96	1996-97	1997-98	1999-00	2000-01	2001-02
RMs/Net Sales	0.6097415	0.624609933	0.5988969	0.5670874	0.538023	0.526926	0.4965461	0.4648505	0.4574887
W&S/Net Sales	0.0701918	0.063918126	0.05893	0.0681017	0.070473	0.066022	0.0789923	0.0827872	0.0828203
P&F/Net Sales	0.0275897	0.027476596	0.0268064	0.0227505	0.024486	0.025532	0.0260158	0.0267404	0.0291418
Adv/Net Sales	0.0305254	0.026445232	0.0257694	0.0557666	0.048257	0.052919	0.0538399	0.0453763	0.0512859

TABLE 1.6- FINANCIAL RATIOS FOR COTTON TEXTILES

Variables	1990-91	1991-92	1992-93	1995-96	1996-97	1997-98	1999-00	2000-01	2001-02
RMs/Net Sales	0.561228	0.605996	0.597878	0.6654535	0.61551	0.631946	0.613425	0.62243	0.616703
W&S/Net Sales	0.175441	0.15915335	0.141654	0.0927826	0.097569	0.108749	0.099302	0.095323	0.096897
P&F/Net Sales	0.092292	0.08731345	0.086317	0.0743795	0.081264	0.089837	0.091552	0.099298	0.096514
Adv/Net Sales	0.002722	0.00228587	0.002285	0.0032561	0.003062	0.00323	0.004849	0.003153	0.003206

TABLE 1.7- FINANCIAL RATIOS FOR SYNTHETIC TEXTILES

Variables	1990-91	1991-92	1992-93	1995-96	1996-97	1997-98	1999-00	2000-01	2001-02
RMs/Net Sales	0.558573	0.57789227	0.003089	0.6919479	0.682553	0.692027	0.702909	0.711201	0.676719
W&S/Net Sales	0.069591	0.06349434	0.059887	0.0644378	0.065517	0.069551	0.067877	0.062328	0.676719
P&F/Net Sales	0.098493	0.09415477	0.089262	0.090747	0.094291	0.099292	0.100311	0.100726	0.09634
Adv/Net Sales	0.003863	0.00308921	0.002447	0.0015679	0.001436	0.001395	0.001115	0.001112	0.001318

TABLE 1.8- FINANCIAL RATIOS FOR INORGANIC CHEMICALS

Variables	1990-91	1991-92	1992-93	1995-96	1996-97	1997-98	1999-00	2000-01	2001-02
RMs/Net Sales	0.528314	0.51738	0.53919694	0.559871	0.5131263	0.496128	0.472454	0.457329	0.484877
W&S/Net Sales	0.079344	0.082888	0.07384139	0.073379	0.0840885	0.102617	0.10624	0.104312	0.102649
P&F/Net Sales	0.139867	0.130348	0.12801602	0.138143	0.1589152	0.185272	0.194039	0.191511	0.202772
Adv/Net Sales	0.001298	0.002005	0.001821	0.012193	0.0153918	0.016024	0.000406	0.00045	0.020573

TABLE 1.9- FINANCIAL RATIOS FOR ALKALIES

Variables	1990-91	1991-92	1992-93	1995-96	1996-97	1997-98	1999-00	2000-01	2001-02
RMs/Net Sales	0.2687147	0.2746029	0.234102768	0.27394	0.2848091	0.298965	0.4356659	0.3854746	0.3848043
W&S/Net Sales	0.0599373	0.0606171	0.053418236	0.074615	0.0861915	0.093557	0.0902474	0.0945323	0.0791161
P&F/Net Sales	0.2896552	0.2677561	0.262580702	0.301561	0.3234016	0.368811	0.347077	0.3749131	0.3431092
Adv/Net Sales	0.0016301	0.000639	0.00035376	0.000387	0.0004713	0.000376	9.214E-05	8.693 E-05	0.0004547

TABLE 1.10- FINANCIAL RATIOS FOR FERTILIZERS

Variables	1990-91	1991-92	1992-93	1995-96	1996-97	1997-98	1999-00	2000-01	2001-02
RMs/Net Sales	0.495304	0.60635902	0.58358	0.59203	0.537506	0.564361	0.602114	0.597008	0.578992
W&S/Net Sales	0.050367	0.04676732	0.050479	0.060472	0.058472	0.05564	0.060605	0.058909	0.058015
P&F/Net Sales	0.126939	0.11269375	0.13096	0.125697	0.13485	0.13746	0.149015	0.155468	0.1377667
Adv/Net Sales	0.001719	0.00159938	0.001593	0.0018158	0.002233	0.002138	0.002027	0.001106	0.0009311

TABLE 1.11- FINANCIAL RATIOS FOR PESTICIDES

Variables	1990-91	1991-92	1992-93	1995-96	1996-97	1997-98	1999-00	2000-01	2001-02
RMs/Net Sales	0.591815	0.591102	0.57125085	0.630023	0.6195937	0.571434	0.564866	0.585353	0.570839
W&S/Net Sales	0.103463	0.096451	0.09409636	0.082513	0.0704556	0.085352	0.077761	0.077806	0.075772
P&F/Net Sales	0.04659	0.047041	0.04716128	0.043159	0.0448284	0.043119	0.048087	0.049541	0.048266
Adv/Net Sales	0.006716	0.005943	0.00486315	0.011282	0.0108896	0.013297	0.013387	0.01375	0.009867

TABLE 1.12- FINANCIAL RATIOS FOR PAINTS AND VARNISHES

Variables	1990-91	1991-92	1992-93	1995-96	1996-97	1997-98	1999-00	2000-01	2001-02
RMs/Net Sales	0.658036	0.64919971	0.623422	0.6710936	0.621614	0.603859	0.600212	0.602803	0.559212
W&S/Net Sales	0.069614	0.06432868	0.069269	0.0631251	0.063603	0.064504	0.060149	0.062685	0.068582
P&F/Net Sales	0.011114	0.00988888	0.010469	0.0135586	0.015689	0.016222	0.014718	0.013983	0.014787
Adv/Net Sales	0.015144	0.0162096	0.013502	0.0212269	0.02083	0.021597	0.02425	0.028189	0.031785

TABLE 1.13- FINANCIAL RATIOS FOR DYES AND PIGMENTS

Variables	1990-91	1991-92	1992-93	1995-96	1996-97	1997-98	1999-00	2000-01	2001-02
RMs/Net Sales	0.6161047	0.5865907	0.59107349	0.651505	0.6051013	0.602853	0.573456	0.642266	0.66084
W&S/Net Sales	0.0993511	0.0983532	0.102193151	0.084212	0.0881272	0.091349	0.0954154	0.0813419	0.0800547
P&F/Net Sales	0.0863738	0.0879479	0.090342439	0.068523	0.0793945	0.088228	0.1000385	0.0932248	0.0930862
Adv/Net Sales	0.0013828	0.0017191	0.001846864	0.001764	0.0014554	0.001852	0.0009952	0.0011161	0.0010885

TABLE 1.14- FINANCIAL RATIOS FOR DRUGS AND PHARMACEUTICALS

Variables	1990-91	1991-92	1992-93	1995-96	1996-97	1997-98	1999-00	2000-01	2001-02
RMs/Net Sales	0.58396	0.61340581	0.61566	0.0599524	0.591765	0.56566	0.5750616	0.5653046	0.5354312
W&S/Net Sales	0.1212607	0.114151184	0.1016094	0.0915941	0.089178	0.094659	0.0889542	0.0894132	0.0871376
P&F/Net Sales	0.0369054	0.036868705	0.0359086	0.0340753	0.033922	0.034545	0.0354014	0.0328364	0.0288609
Adv/Net Sales	0.0134012	0.012362288	0.0133177	0.0118315	0.011253	0.014198	0.0121675	0.0125091	0.0114524

TABLE 1.15- FINANCIAL RATIOS FOR SOAPS AND DETERGENTS

Variables	1990-91	1991-92	1992-93	1995-96	1996-97	1997-98	1999-00	2000-01	2001-02
RMs/Net Sales	0.692477	0.70583725	0.703948	0.7185809	0.711063	0.712265	0.69862	0.732702	0.658435
W&S/Net Sales	0.068713	0.05179079	0.052659	0.059066	0.057448	0.055581	0.057308	0.059366	0.057524
P&F/Net Sales	0.029795	0.02619892	0.028773	0.0243072	0.034753	0.033649	0.045631	0.058987	0.059191
Adv/Net Sales	0.029256	0.02731717	0.038771	0.0284658	0.02728	0.033495	0.031058	0.050171	0.049541

TABLE 1.16- FINANCIAL RATIOS FOR COSMETICS AND TOILETRIES

Variables	1990-91	1991-92	1992-93	1995-96	1996-97	1997-98	1999-00	2000-01	2001-02
RMs/Net Sales	0.653368	0.665167	0.63521585	0.216437	0.2136854	0.211051	0.558184	0.537849	0.536334
W&S/Net Sales	0.058837	0.057795	0.05738263	0.611506	0.5985583	0.575399	0.367777	0.059342	0.065636
P&F/Net Sales	0.007577	0.008133	0.00892115	0.051407	0.047759	0.053944	0.012015	0.012887	0.012523
Adv/Net Sales	0.059903	0.057536	0.06736221	0.111033	0.1131457	0.138303	0.128971	0.123888	0.124357

TABLE 1.17- FINANCIAL RATIOS FOR ORGANIC CHEMICALS

Variables	1990-91	1991-92	1992-93	1995-96	1996-97	1997-98	1999-00	2000-01	2001-02
RMs/Net Sales	0.5085179	0.5192976	0.562169947	0.551842	0.559883	0.603643	0.5944261	0.6081591	0.5797171
W&S/Net Sales	0.0597104	0.0549764	0.054995466	0.050711	0.0558116	0.057146	0.0590441	0.0572638	0.0583738
P&F/Net Sales	0.1050256	0.096488	0.10849736	0.086147	0.1016313	0.101758	0.1061341	0.1146943	0.1071228
Adv/Net Sales	0.0005963	0.0003723	0.000480077	0.000726	0.0005796	0.000408	0.000211	0.0002502	0.0002917

TABLE 1.18- FINANCIAL RATIOS FOR POYMERS

Variables	1990-91	1991-92	1992-93	1995-96	1996-97	1997-98	1999-00	2000-01	2001-02
RMs/Net Sales	0.484077	0.519034	0.51451195	0.469093	0.4841254	0.548698	0.584659	0.582841	0.561354
W&S/Net Sales	0.066	0. 063897	0.06847782	0.079135	0.0739759	0.079124	0.067319	0.06918	0.084395
P&F/Net Sales	0.101491	0.087019	0.10498294	0.078426	0.0882171	0.113561	0.102918	0.111606	0.103937
Adv/Net Sales	0.00235	0.003225	0.00415017	0.003101	0.0034926	0.002788	0.002937	0.002265	0.003233

TABLE 1.19 FINANCIAL RATIOS FOR PLASTIC PRODUCTS

Variables	1990-91	1991-92	1992-93	1995-96	1996-97	1997-98	1999-00	2000-01	2001-02
RMs/Net Sales	0.6748481	0.694051153	0.6753564	0.7134296	0.700551	0.681587	0.6555461	0.6657564	0.6458991
W&S/Net Sales	0.0618874	0.05446449	0.0568258	0.0438006	0.049916	0.050404	0.0559141	0.0558014	0.0591037
P&F/Net Sales	0.0329688	0.029915506	0.0334832	0.0306844	0.039395	0.048502	0.057815	0.0565279	0.05741
Adv/Net Sales	0.0042932	0.005309431	0.0053573	0.0053253	0.005027	0.000528	0.0048727	0.0049909	0.0051388

TABLE 1.20- FINANCIAL RATIOS FOR PETROLEUM PRODUCTS

Variables	1990-91	1991-92	1992-93	1995-96	1996-97	1997-98	1999-00	2000-01	2001-02
RMs/Net Sales	0.7906082	0.742090731	0.7374511	0.7920885	0.779245	0.796844	0.913415	0.8839026	0.8655503
W&S/Net Sales	0.0132356	0.013452341	0.0129921	0.0172623	0.012593	0.016036	0.0141463	0.0142481	0.0159803
P&F/Net Sales	0.013555	0.012692449	0.011563	0.0091912	0.008665	0.010333	0.0209511	0.0179142	0.0211721
Adv/Net Sales	0.0001793	0.000170537	0.0001987	0.0004907	0.000484	0.001109	0.0004537	0.0004378	0.0005346

TABLE 1.21- FINANCIAL RATIOS FOR TYRES AND TUBES

Variables	1990-91	1991-92	1992-93	1995-96	1996-97	1997-98	1999-2000	2000-01	2001-02
RMs/Net Sales	0.6467457	0.65589884	0.6604277	0.6669491	0.689531	0.616957	0.6076825	0.6401374	0.6110995
W&S/Net Sales	0.0745294	0.075009777	0.0753916	0.0643442	0.068553	0.073744	0.0789517	0.088914	0.0824029
P&F/Net Sales	0.040275	0.042836658	0.0490928	0.0397299	0.045965	0.049145	0.0579398	0.0629679	0.0550791
Adv/Net Sales	0.0134356	0.013661843	0.0132329	0.0108379	0.011341	0.013516	0.0179796	0.0128766	0.0128121

TABLE 1.22 – FINANCIAL RATIOS FOR RUBBER AND RUBBER PRODUCTS

Variables	1990-91	1991-92	1992-93	1995-96	1996-97	1997-98	1999-2000	2000-01	2001-02
RMs/Net Sales	0.5769588	0.573074317	0.5767918	0.572654	0.522241	0.523658	0.5107412	0.507647	0.4983852
W&S/Net Sales	0.1529885	0.152021685	0.1463562	0.1274192	0.1246	0.152862	0.1606119	0.1512405	0.1576024
P&F/Net Sales	0.0922886	0.074090806	0.0692632	0.0602573	0.062848	0.075092	0.0827803	0.0871191	0.0824183
Adv/Net Sales	0.0012388	0.0025258866	0.0054206	0.0025107	0.006908	0.004662	0.0071983	0.0073638	0.0089136

TABLE 1.23- FINANCIAL RATIOS FOR CEMENT

Variables	1990-91	1991-92	1992-93	1995-96	1996-97	1997-98	1999-2000	2000-01	2001-02
RMs/Net Sales	0.2493084	0.254034254	0.2616089	0.2377258	0.249103	0.2333708	0.2512558	0.2422256	0.2397562
W&S/Net Sales	0.0756101	0.066511567	0.0756111	0.0685223	0.077033	0.08072	0.0780763	0.0708486	0.0692191
P&F/Net Sales	0.2444522	0.252235752	0.2821373	0.2688526	0.299525	0.321506	0.3221247	0.2875858	0.2807741
Adv/Net Sales	0.0025	0.002838	0.003251	0.006171	0.006078	0.006572	0.181636	0.008189	0.007098

TABLE 1.24 FINANCIAL RATIOS FOR PIG AND SPONGE IRON

Variables	1990-91	1991-92	1992-93	1995-96	1996-97	1997-98	1999-2000	2000-01	2001-02
RMs/Net Sales	0.578941	0.49924046	0.572249	0.6402844	0.637211	0.673688	0.600986	0.642544	0.658553
W&S/Net Sales	0.211136	0.02332231	0.020818	0.0253288	0.027871	0.032875	0.046226	0.046406	0.043785
P&F/Net Sales	0.059969	0.06147797	0.073757	0.0735233	0.89105	0.080449	0.062101	0.06581	0.068818
Adv/Net Sales	0.000637	0.00035743	0.011492	0.0012548	0.000554	0.000481	0.000623	0.000271	0.00039

TABLE 1.25 FINANCIAL RATIOS FOR STEEL

Variables	1990-91	1991-92	1992-93	1995-96	1996-97	1997-98	1999-2000	2000-01	2001-02
RMs/Net Sales	0.536249	0.5583101	0.584550436	0.584635	0.6174128	0.614345	0.5753433	0.5906622	0.6046973
W&S/Net Sales	0.1177545	0.1144886	0.110199407	0.109206	0.1095469	0.112754	0.1168308	0.1167747	0.1233554
P&F/Net Sales	0.0882475	0.0856525	0.093406988	0.092487	0.1105658	0.111319	0.114755	0.1139082	0.1187011
Adv/Net Sales	0.0002164	0.0001556	0.000166173	0.000394	0.0002587	0.000133	0.0001186	0.0001156	0.0001158

TABLE 1.26 FINANCIAL RATIOS FOR FERRO ALLOYS

Variables	1990-91	1991-92	1992-93	1995-96	1996-97	1997-98	1999-2000	2000-01	2001-02
RMs/Net Sales	0.4446757	0.4559322	0.434643464	0.474761	.4156724	0.451436	0.4634918	0.4425044	0.4535133
W&S/Net Sales	0.0915713	0.074092	0.073107311	0.060285	0.0767454	0.085046	0.0941381	0.0785732	0.0861198
P&F/Net Sales	0.3407908	0.2771186	0.324632463	0.276775	0.3174505	0.312412	0.3169053	0.3040659	0.2938733
Adv/Net Sales	0.0001734	0.0002421	0.00030003	0.000262	0.0002309	0.000157	0.0001582	0.0001247	0.0001385

TABLE 1.27 FINANCIAL RATIOS FOR CASTINGS AND FORGINGS

Variables	1990-91	1991-92	1992-93	1995-96	1996-97	1997-98	1999-2000	2000-01	2001-02
RMs/Net Sales	0.609848	0.5912388	0.600808407	0.661862	0.6889361	0.661066	0.6247408	0.6077007	0.6090202
W&S/Net Sales	0.1043161	0.0998262	0.096928052	0.073181	0.0779845	0.08555	0.075724	0.0680731	0.0638565
P&F/Net Sales	0.0826748	0.0858274	0.094260307	0.078835	0.08248	0.093219	0.1044691	0.1029454	0.0955338
Adv/Net Sales	0.0003647	0.0003862	0.000485044	0.001553	0.0009366	0.000533	0.0005005	0.0004611	0.0005645

TABLE 1.28- FINANCIAL RATIOS FOR METAL PRODUCTS

Variables	1990-91	1991-92	1992-93	1995-96	1996-97	1997-98	1999-2000	2000-01	2001-02
RMs/Net Sales	0.663077	0.6418736	0.667524	0.6759014	0.64303	0.640917	0.612189	0.610859	0.607835
W&S/Net Sales	0.089545	0.0860237	0.08145	0.0633705	0.065269	0.070995	0.078049	0.077248	0.073406
P&F/Net Sales	0.42448	0.04721842	0.047982	0.0454844	0.054202	0.054163	0.054415	0.052608	0.05208
Adv/Net Sales	0.001364	0.001876312	0.00199	0.0023018	0.00197	0.001868	0.002781	0.00625	0.004197

TABLE 1.29 FINANCIAL RATIOS FOR NON FERROUS METALS

Variables	1990-91	1991-92	1992-93	1995-96	1996-97	1997-98	1999-2000	2000-01	2001-02
RMs/Net Sales	0.3867279	0.388283852	0.4193013	0.46161	0.478768	0.440519	0.4955618	0.4674532	0.5116583
W&S/Net Sales	0.0988862	0.094358513	0.099991	0.0799022	0.092872	0.09501	0.0965447	0.0854019	0.0920656
P&F/Net Sales	0.1897706	0.181013874	0.1760766	0.1334128	0149492	0.165121	0.145469	0.1399514	0.1357405
Adv/Net Sales	0.000321	0.00032692	0.001083	0.0006163	0.000493	0.000464	0.000315	0.000301	0.000231

TABLE 1.30 - FINANCIAL RATIOS FOR NON ELECTRICAL MACHINERY

Variables	1990-91	1991-92	1992-93	1995-96	1996-97	1997-98	1999-2000	2000-01	2001-02
RMs/Net Sales	0.6190476	0.615137085	0.597148	0.5945871	0.575478	0.559961	0.5589842	0.5815215	0.5670936
W&S/Net Sales	0.1371727	0.1328939	0.1259741	0.140692	0.126618	0.134058	0.1474451	0.1929297	0.1582729
P&F/Net Sales	0.0182804	0.017776278	0.0187908	0.0204862	0.021156	0.022546	0.0242895	0.0255857	0.0237006
Adv/Net Sales	0.0031684	0.0016868	0.0018576	0.0023846	0.002023	0.001898	0.00194	0.0023993	0.0020423

TABLE 1.31 FINANCIAL RATIOS FOR ELECTRICAL MACHINERY

Variables	1990-91	1991-92	1992-93	1995-96	1996-97	1997-98	1999-2000	2000-01	2001-02
RMs/Net Sales	0.633434	0.609783587	0.6103948	0.6712294	0.637672	0.617106	0.6193337	0.629266	0.6387686
W&S/Net Sales	0.1308463	0.124496851	0.1215927	0.0876829	0.097111	0.101868	0.0997359	0.0918357	0.0900518
P&F/Net Sales	0.0254927	0.025486575	0.0270197	0.021783	0.02441	0.028712	0.0292681	0.0304859	0.0270661
Adv/Net Sales	0.0039589	0.003930483	0.0039564	0.0123057	0.010812	0.013571	0.0109761	0.0129191	0.0113629

TABLE 1.32 - FINANCIAL RATIOS FOR ELECTRONICS

Variables	1990-91	1991-92	1992-93	1995-96	1996-97	1997-98	1999-2000	2000-01	2001-02
RMs/Net Sales	0.6478948	0.625726207	0.6453888	0.6775213	0.610022	0.580733	0.5030671	0.4482442	0.4154089
W&S/Net Sales	0.111606	0.103187388	0.1087477	0.0965952	0.09573	0.109192	0.1269807	0.1451356	0.1752459
P&F/Net Sales	0.0102697	0.010351748	0.0111614	0.0101874	0.010295	0.010512	0.0094589	0.0087887	0.0092811
Adv/Net Sales	0.008785	0.008608852	0.0107136	0.0192111	0.017066	0.015314	0.0096459	0.0124056	0.0094202

TABLE 1.33 FINANCIAL RATIOS FOR TRANSPORT EQUIPMENT

Variables	1990-91	1991-92	1992-93	1995-96	1996-97	1997-98	1999-2000	2000-01	2001-02
RMs/Net Sales	0.6536449	0.650528181	0.6816436	0.6696744	0.668297	0.632862	0.6326707	0.6673167	0.653561
W&S/Net Sales	0.129231	0.12106231	0.128719	0.099144	0.093587	0.103481	0.097092	0.097209	0.087562
P&F/Net Sales	0.0207901	0.020572681	0.0237007	0.0225851	0.023437	0.025206	0.0238775	0.0249973	0.0231342
Adv/Net Sales	0.0042408	0.004105068	0.0049853	0.0050837	0.005776	0.008093	0.0097316	0.0125827	0.0127782

TABLE 1.34 - FINANCIAL RATIOS FOR AUTOMOBILE

Variables	1990-91	1991-92	1992-93	1995-96	1996-97	1997-98	1999-2000	2000-01	2001-02
RMs/Net Sales	0.0734952	0.666518869	0.7087741	0.70015360	0.697593	0.656974	0.6525286	0.696723	0.6830893
W&S/Net Sales	0.014128	0.12022531	0.1301937	0.0990419	0.090225	0.099107	0.0906991	0.091283	0.0773103
P&F/Net Sales	0.0021277	0.018819588	0.0219961	0.0178892	0.018265	0.019465	0.0173786	0.0180794	0.0159231
Adv/Net Sales	0.0004918	0.004433934	0.0058347	0.0059301	0.006953	0.009899	0.0120763	0.016374	0.0167801

TABLE 1.35 FINANCIAL RATIOS FOR AUTOMOBILE ANCILLIARIES

Variables	1990-91	1991-92	1992-93	1995-96	1996-97	1997-98	1999-2000	2000-01	2001-02
RMs/Net Sales	0.5754798	0.5758494	0.572747904	0.569745	0.5730696	0.557175	0.5666923	0.5850158	0.5736306
W&S/Net Sales	0.1338431	0.1249712	0.122801488	0.099478	0.1045148	0.117213	0.1183343	0.1137946	0.1152862
P&F/Net Sales	0.0287132	0.0287599	0.030542772	0.037981	0.040244	0.043226	0.0454793	0.0443599	0.0426314
Adv/Net Sales	0.0029878	0.0026076	0.001575994	0.00232	0.0019403	0.00242	0.0019485	0.0019713	0.0019578

TABLE 1.36 - FINANCIAL RATIOS FOR PAPER AND PAPER PRODUCTS

Variables	1990-91	1991-92	1992-93	1995-96	1996-97	1997-98	1999-2000	2000-01	2001-02
RMs/Net Sales	0.4456041	0.460108164	0.4751054	0.4728876	0.476886	0.486959	0.4783556	0.4799757	0.4887779
W&S/Net Sales	0.091096	0.090394025	0.0896298	0.0766597	0.083404	0.087665	0.0933764	0.0867593	0.0881469
P&F/Net Sales	0.1876441	0.195106876	0.2019524	0.1683719	0.213592	0.219032	0.201619	0.1780335	0.1799575
Adv/Net Sales	0.000405	0.000386299	0.0004427	0.0018079	0.000788	0.000661	0.0005103	0.0004426	0.0003814

TABLE 1.37 FINANCIAL RATIOS FOR LEATHER PRODUCTS

Variables	1990-91	1991-92	1992-93	1995-96	1996-97	1997-98	1999-2000	2000-01	2001-02
RMs/Net Sales	0.6029412	0.578329484	0.6093294	0.7148231	0.068064	0.657888	0.6338942	0.655875	0.5987525
W&S/Net Sales	0.200692	0.19495766	0.1631119	0.110556	0.010566	0.112359	0.12730777	0.1251528	0.1471841
P&F/Net Sales	0.0222751	0.020592764	0.0170324	0.0140473	0.001515	0.01825	0.0219231	0.0235001	0.0269298
Adv/Net Sales	0.0129758	0.013471901	0.0105877	0.0103444	0.000776	0.007794	0.0094712	0.0082409	0.0136148

TABLE 1.38 - FINANCIAL RATIOS FOR BOOKS AND NEWSPAPERS

Variables	1990-91	1991-92	1992-93	1995-96	1996-97	1997-98	1999-2000	2000-01	2001-02
RMs/Net Sales	0.513568	0.489401	0.450378	0.491126	0.4686543	0.451216	0.418662	0.456772	0.466199
W&S/Net Sales	0.135859	0.129542	0.12819688	0.102139	0.1187094	0.116696	0.120402	0.112643	0.110539
P&F/Net Sales	0.010381	0.009253	0.01029435	0.009168	0.0104077	0.011766	0.012248	0.012879	0.013064
Adv/Net Sales	0.005463	0.006057	0.00466463	0.005936	0.0224685	0.028601	0.014512	0.013435	0.014556

TABLE 1.39 FINANCIAL RATIOS FOR WOOD

Variables	1990-91	1991-92	1992-93	1995-96	1996-97	1997-98	1999-2000	2000-01	2001-02
RMs/Net Sales	0.5949787	0.612550607	0.617388	0.5435015	0.539793	0.609474	0.5925727	0.6045651	0.582027
W&S/Net Sales	0.081478	0.079352227	0.0877059	0.0711236	0.077003	0.078578	0.0876793	0.0862431	0.1021263
P&F/Net Sales	0.0558977	0.056275304	0.0658751	0.0539098	0.063953	0.062788	0.0816463	0.0782233	0.0841223
Adv/Net Sales	0.0075793	0.005668016	0.0049789	0.0168135	0.010465	0.009325	0.0128704	0.0096237	0.0116405

TABLE 1.40 - FINANCIAL RATIOS FOR CLOCKS AND WATCHES

Variables	1990-91	1991-92	1992-93	1995-96	1996-97	1997-98	1999-2000	2000-01	2001-02
RMs/Net Sales	0.6841104	0.5881963	0.543628014	0.539004	0.6081487	0.463815	0.5463542	0.5547741	0.5403742
W&S/Net Sales	0.0666032	0.061008	0.082663605	0.090103	0.1175366	0.115683	0.131713	0.1294293	0.2088111
P&F/Net Sales	3.0980019	2.566313	3.399540758	0.011893	0.0144574	0.016964	1.185708	1.0987287	0.8107423
Adv/Net Sales	0.079924	0.062997	0.07577497	0.082645	0.0837401	0.04584	0.072479	0.063971	0.054315

TABLE 1.41 - FINANCIAL RATIOS FOR DIVERSIFIED

Variables	1990-91	1991-92	1992-93	1995-96	1996-97	1997-98	1999-2000	2000-01	2001-02
RMs/Net Sales	0.584131	0.592704 39	0.576914	0.5912126	0.596514	0.620777	0.619361	0.635284	0.736885
W&S/Net Sales	0.123722	0.116076 09	0.107758	0.0830828	0.080255	0.077688	0.073527	0.062589	0.046104
P&F/Net Sales	0.065141	0.070382 86	0.082088	0.081111	0.078937	0.07655	0.069654	0.072428	0.049513
Adv/Net Sales	0.007315	0.006742 62	0.006346	0.0071143	0.0127	0.015986	0.016856	0.014843	0.011303

BIBLIOGRAPHY

Books

- Ahluwalia, I. J. (1991). *Productivity and Growth of Indian Manufacturing.* Delhi: Oxford University Press.
- Basu, Kaushik. (2004). Indian Economy: Up To 1991 and Since. In Kaushik, Basu. *India's Emerging Economy: Performance and Prospects in the 1990s and Beyond.* Cmabridge: MIT Press.
- Bhagwati, Jagdish. (1993). India *in Transition Freeing the Economy.* Oxford: Clarendon Press.
- Bhagwati, Jagdish and Padma, Desai. (1970). *India Planning For Industrialization.* London: Oxford University Press.
- Brahmananda, P.R. and V.R. Panchamukhi. (1987). *The Development Process of The Indian Economy.* New Delhi: Himalaya Publishing House.
- Chandra, Satish and Mala Chandra. (1997). *Privatization of Public Enterprises: A Constitutional Anatomy.* New Delhi: Deep and Deep Publications.
- Degnbol- Martnussen John. (2001). *Institutions and Industrial Development - Coping With Liberalisation and International Competition in India.* New Delhi: Sage Publications.
- Desai, S. S. M. (1988). *Industrial Economy of India.* Bombay: Himalaya Publishing House.
- Goswami, Omkar and Rakesh, Mohan. (I996). Industry: An Unfinished Agenda. In Vijay. L. Kelkar and V .V Bhanoji Rao. *India Development Policy Imperatives.* New Delhi: Tata McGraw-Hill Publishing Company Limited.
- Gupta, K. R. (ed). (2000). *Liberalisation and Globalization of Indian Economy.* Volume I. New Delhi: Atlantic Publishers and Distributors.
- Kapila, Uma, (ed). (2001-02). *Indian Economy since Independence.* Delhi: Academic Foundation.
- Kansra, S.L. and Rajeev Jain. (1999). Challenges and Opportunities under the New Economic Policy and Response of Indian Private Corporate Sector: An Assessment. In P.P.Arya and B.B.Tandon. (eds). *Multinationals versus Swadeshi Today: A Policy Framework for Economic Nationalism.* New Delhi: Deep and Deep Publications.
- Kathuria, Sanjay (1995). Competitiveness of Indian Industry. In Dilip Mookherjee (ed). *Indian Industry: Policies and Performance.* New Delhi: Oxford University Press.

- Meier, Gerald M. (1995). *Leading Issues in Economic Development*, Delhi: Oxford University Press.
- Palande, P.S. (2000). *Coping with Liberalisation- The Industry's Response to New Competition*. New Delhi: Response Books.
- Seth, Vijay. K. (1999). *Capacity Utilisation in Industries Theory and Evidence.* New Delhi: Deep and Deep Publications.
- Srivastava, Vivek. (1996). *Liberalization, Productivity and Competition: A Panel Study of Indian Manufacturing.* New Delhi: Oxford University Press.
- Thirlwal, A.P. (1989). *Growth and Development with Special Reference to Developing Economies.* London: English Language Book Society/Macmillan..

Dictionary

- New Palgrave (1987). A Dictionary of Economics. London: Macmillan.

Newspaper Items

- The Economic Times. May 5. 2003.
- The Economic Times. May 29. 2003
- The Economic Times. July 8. 2003.
- The Economic Times. September 30. 2015.

Papers

- Bhaumik, Sumon Kumar and Kumhakar, Subal, C. (2008). Impact of Reforms on Plant-Level Productivity and Technical Efficiency: Evidence from the Indian Manufacturing Sector. *IZA*. Discussion Paper No. 3347, February, accessed from: http://www.sumonbhaumik.net/iza_dp3347.pdf, visited on February 10, 2016.
- Eliot. (1971). Social Control of Private Business. *Economic and Political Weekly.* Volume VI (30-32), July, pp. 1697-1702.
- Ghosh, Arabinda. (1975). Concentration and Growth of Indian Industries 1948-68. *Journal of Industrial Economics*, Volume XXIII (3), March, pp. 203- 222.
- Gokarn, Subir. (2001). The State of Indian Industry. Downloaded from: http://www.india-seminar.com/2001/507/507%20subir%20gokarn.htm, visited on February, 10, 2016.
- Goldar, B.N. (1986). Productivity trends in the Indian Manufacturing industry, 1951-1978. *Indian Economic Review*. Volume 28 (1), pp. 73-94.

- Gupta, Vinod. K. (1968). Cost functions, Concentration and Barriers to Entry in Twenty Nine manufacturing industries of India. *Journal of Industrial Economics.*Volume 26. November, pp.57-72.
- Harberger, Arnold. C. (1959). The Fundamentals of Economic Progress in Underdeveloped Countries- Using the Resources At Hand More Effectively. *American Economic Review*, Volume XLIX (2), May, pp.134-146.
- Jeemol Unni, N. Lalitha and Uma Rani. (2001). Economic Reforms and Productivity in Indian Manufacturing. *Economic and Political Weekly.* Volume. 36, No. 41, October 13-19. pp.3914-3922.
- Kabra, Kamal Nayan. (2002). A Decade Of Reforms: The Unfinished Agenda. The Theme Paper for the Members' Annual Conference of the IIPA. New Delhi.
- Kansra, S.L. (1999). Challenges of Globalisation and Indian Corporate Sector - An Assessment of Response. *Social Science Research Journal.* Volume 7 (3), Panjab University, Chandigarh, pp. 77-97.
- Kathuria, Vinish, Raj, Rajesh, S, N and Sen, Kunal. (2013). Productivity Measurement in Indian Manufacturing: A Comparison of Alternative Methods. *Journal of Quantitative Economics*. Volume 11 (1 &2), January – July. Accessed from: http://www.jqe.co.in/journals/jqe_v11_148-179_vinish_kathuria.pdf, visited on February 10, 2016.
- Kelkar, Vijay. K., and Kumar, Rajiv. (1990). Industrial Growth In the Eighties Emerging Policy Issues. *Economic and Political Weekly*. Special Articles. January 27, pp. 209-222.
- Khatkhate, D. (1992). The Regulatory Impediments to the Private Industrial Sector Development in Asia: A Comparative Study. *World Bank Discussion Paper* Number-177, Washington D C.
- Klein, L.R. (1960). Some Theoretical Issues in the Measurement of Capacity Utilization. *Econometrica.* Volume 28 (2), pp. 272-86.
- Kurien, C.T. (1989). Indian Economy in the 1980s and on to the 1990s. *Economic and Political Weekly. Special Articles*. Volume XXIV (15), April 15, pp. 787-798.
- Nayyar, Deepak. (1998). Economic Development and Political Democracy- Interaction of Economics and Politics in Independent India. *Economic and Political Weekly*. Volume 33. December 5, pp. 3 126-3127.
- Patibandla, M. and Phani, B.V. (2002). Market Reforms and Industrial Productivity: An Explanation, *Economic and Political Weekly*. Volume 37(1), January, pp. 59.

- Rangarajan, C. (2001-02). Economic Reforms: Some Issues and Concerns. *The Indian Economic Journal.* Volume 49 (2). Special Number in Industrial Economics. October-December, pp. 1-6.
- Raut, Lakshmi K. (2002-03). The Effect of Competitiveness and Productivity Growth on Exports of Indian Private Firms. *Indian Economic Journal.* Volume 50 (3 and 4), pp. 48-62.
- Sawhey, P.K. and Sawhey, B.L. (1973). Capacity Utilisation Concentration and Price-Cost Margins: Results on Indian Industry, *Journal of Industrial Economics.* Volume 21, April.
- Siggel, Eckhard. (2001). India's Trade Policy Reforms and Industry Competitiveness in the 1980 's. *World Economy.* Volume 24, pp 159-183.

Ph.D. Dissertation

- Kansra, S.L. (1990). *Monopoly Power: Some Aspects of its Impact in Indian Industry* (1950-1966). Department of Economics, Panjab University. Chandigarh.

Reports/Surveys

- Bandyopadhyay, M. (2009).Policies and Programmes for Industrial Development and Innovation in India. *ASB-RETA final Report.* Downloaded from: www.namstct.org/ACB_RETA_Report/Mr. M.Bandyopadhyay.pdf, visited on February 10, 2016.
- Global Competitiveness Report. (2003-04). *World Economic Forum.* Downloaded from: www.weforum.com, visited on February 10, 2016.
- Indian Council of Social Science Research. (1975). A Survey of Research in Economics- Industry. Volume V. New Delhi: Allied Publishers.
- Industry Outlook (various years). *CMIE.* Mumbai.